Creating A Room

Also by Charlotte Moss

A Passion for Detail

Creating A Room

A Guide to Decorating Your Home in Stages

Charlotte Moss

ILLUSTRATIONS BY
James Steinmeyer

PENGUIN
STUDIO

PENGUIN STUDIO
Published by the Penguin Group
Penguin Books USA Inc., 375 Hudson Street,
New York, New York 10014, U.S.A.
Penguin Books Ltd, 27 Wrights Lane,
London W8 5TZ, England
Penguin Books Australia Ltd, Ringwood,
Victoria, Australia
Penguin Books Canada Ltd, 10 Alcorn Avenue,
Toronto, Ontario, Canada M4V 3B2
Penguin Books (N.Z.) Ltd, 182–190 Wairau Road,
Auckland 10, New Zealand

Penguin Books Ltd, Registered Offices:
Harmondsworth, Middlesex, England

First published in 1995 by Viking Penguin,
a division of Penguin Books USA Inc.

5 7 9 10 8 6 4

Copyright © Charlotte Moss, 1995
Illustrations copyright © James Steinmeyer, 1995
All rights reserved

Photographs by D. James Dee

ISBN 0–670–84799–2
Cataloging-in-Publication data available

Printed in Hong Kong
Set in Galliard
Designed by Barbara Scott-Goodman

ACKNOWLEDGMENTS

Thank you, thank you . . .

to the hundreds of people who have attended my lectures and talks around the country and who time and again have asked the questions "How do you know where to start when you decorate a room?" "What if you don't have the money to do it all at once?" "How did you know how to arrange things that way?" and on and on. All of you are the inspiration behind this book.

Additionally, I am forever grateful to . . .

Jimmy Steinmeyer, the illustrator of the book, for his brilliant interpretation of the room collages and the jumble of notes I gave him. Words almost seem superfluous with Jimmy's amazingly precise drawings

Phyllis Wender, my agent and friend, who keeps me on track and on time

David Easton, for his encouragement, support, and sense of humor

Daphne Carey, my assistant, for taking my often illegible notes and turning them into a text—rewrite after rewrite—and for cataloguing fabrics, artwork, transparencies, and slides

Kristine Kennedy and Megan Ziglar, who researched, edited, proofread, and challenged some points while helping to clarify others

Connie Newberry and Diana Auchincloss, who critiqued my room schemes and who continue to be my resident sounding boards

Gerald Puschel of Schumacher, for being receptive to my idea of using Schumacher fabrics in this book

Marjorie McNaughton of Schumacher, for pulling together endless piles of new fabric strike-offs, and memos and cuttings of many others

Barbara Scott-Goodman, the designer, who shared my vision and who understood from the beginning what this book should look like

Barbara Williams, my editor, for establishing guidelines and for giving sound advice, and for the editing that made this book a better book

Michael Fragnito, for listening to all my ideas and responding to them by sending me away to come back with the proposal that is now this book

My friends, for their encouragement and support and for being constant sources of inspiration and energy

My husband, Barry, for his eternal patience, his abundant support, and his puzzled understanding of my need to write books—he is a husband who has gone from saying, "Why don't you just decorate and forget the books?" to "When is book number three due?" and "What's the subject of number four?"

To each of you—thank you for your contribution to this book.

CONTENTS

*"We shape our dwellings and afterwards,
our dwellings shape us."*

—Winston Churchill

INTRODUCTION

My goal in this book is to demonstrate visually how rooms *do* and *should* evolve slowly over time. Additionally, it is my idea to provide you with a scrapbook of visual information, ideas, and suggestions without burying them in volumes of text. I have read and analyzed a great number of books before deciding to implement this format, and essentially I have put myself in your shoes, asking how you can get the most information in the shortest period of time. By using illustrations I have made it possible for you to visually digest and interpret a decorating idea *your* way.

Some of the principles of interior decoration can be learned from books, but real skill comes from work . . . and more work! Decorating is a little like riding a horse: you must practice in order to learn, and practice even more to become proficient. No amount of reading can substitute for what is learned by doing. There are many great books on interior design, some of which you probably own and cherish. In this book, I have selected a personal approach that will allow you to decorate these rooms with me.

To help you understand the rooms I have created, I will guide you through the process of how to pull all the decorative elements together, from the floor plan to the footstool. Additionally, I will demonstrate that there are always alternative ways of doing things. I have described each room as a certain type of room—that is, naming the use of the room—as opposed to characterizing the room by a particular style. In my nine-year career as an interior decorator, I have never had a client ask me to design a true period room—a relief for me, in a way, because I do not think such rooms are suitable to the way we live today. We may, of course, describe a room as being predominantly French, Italian, American, or Scandinavian, and we might say a room is modern, traditional, formal, or casual. But sometimes rooms defy an easily recognizable style, and I don't want to limit my message to only certain styles of decoration. My techniques are applicable to any type of room, as long as you want to make it comfortable, livable, and suitable to your own needs.

If you asked ten people, "What makes a great room?" you would probably get ten different answers. My definition or formula of what makes a great room has as much to do with the process of creating the room as it does with what furnishes the room. My motto is "Don't try to do it all at once!" In my first book, *A Passion for Detail,* I described three intangible elements that I feel are key in making a great room. Those elements are humor, comfort, and passion. Now I am trying to show how to marry these subtle elements with the more practical elements of patience and planning. Sometimes, waiting until the right thing comes along or until the purse strings have loosened means that you might have to live with more empty space than you would like. But don't feel compelled to fill up a room immediately. I promise you, good things happen to those who wait.

All of us have experienced being in a house where everything seemed to work. You knew that the owner had mastered the art of decorating a room by looking at how she planned the space, the colors, and even more important how she practiced that subtle and skillful art known as accessorizing. Most of us, on the other hand, are constantly seeking to improve our skills via tips, ideas, and new and interesting ways of doing things. If this latter description fits you, I think you will enjoy the experience that is about to unfold.

When I first begin to tackle a decorating project, I divide it into three stages, which I have replicated for the rooms included in this book. Stage I of each room shows the space void of color and containing only the bare essentials, key pieces of furniture, and in most cases, floor coverings. Stage II introduces color, essential lighting, and some key decorative objects to anchor the room. At this stage, some people might consider the room finished, and indeed, it is very livable this way. It is at this point that you may choose to take a breather before going on to the third and final stage. Why? Maybe your budget has been designed that way, or maybe you might want to live in the room for a while to make sure you're on the right track. Settle in, analyze how you use the room, and continue to do your homework. Whatever your reason, you will know when the time is right to move on to Stage III. (To focus on the often less obvious elements of accessorizing implemented in Stage II, I have delayed installing window treatments until the final stage.)

In Stage III, more pictures, additional decorative objects, and additions to fledgling collections are incorporated, giving rooms their completed and lived-in look. Some people refer to this stage as the finished room, and from the standpoint of physical comfort and visual appeal I would agree. But remember that decorating is a process and you must always feel free, even after you have reached the "finished" stage, to change, move, edit, and add to, because evolution is what keeps life in a room. To that end, I have added four variations after Stage III of each room, showing how a particular corner, wall, or piece of furniture could be arranged or accessorized differently. There are alternatives to suit every mood, taste, or decorating style.

Finally, I have included a Dictionary of Details to provide the novice with a visual reference showing a small selection of the many varieties of upholstery details, pillow styles, and lampshade shapes available. Keeping a room fresh, preventing it from becoming static, that is the challenge that awaits you now. Don't be afraid to experiment and try new things.

Do Yourself a favor— Create a Master Plan

When we think about interior decorating, what typically comes to mind is furniture, color, carpets and rugs, window treatments, and the wonderful accessories that give our rooms personality.

Stop. Forget about all those things. That's putting the cart before the horse. I would like for you to think about decorating as a process, not just as the art of filling up rooms with things. You will be doing yourself a great favor if you acknowledge that it is a process, and if you follow a specific five-step plan that I have developed and will outline for you shortly. You will remember the steps of the program easily, using a tip I will also provide. If you follow these five steps, the furniture you select, the colors you choose, and the window treatments you decide on will all be the result of a more focused decision-making process. This plan may even prevent you from making mistakes. Most important, I find that when people follow these five guidelines they often learn things about themselves along the way. All you have to do is use this simple mnemonic device: "Do yourself a favor."

FANTASIZE
ANALYZE
VISUALIZE
OBSERVE
REALIZE

FANTASIZE

Every decorating project begins with an idea, a request, a notion, a dream, or a fantasy of the type of room that is to be created. Inspiration can come from a painting, a room seen in a movie, a museum, a magazine photograph, a description in a novel, a place we've visited, a color that energizes us, and so on. We are surrounded by stimuli every day. You would have to have blinders on to deny it.

Sometimes my clients will express what they want me to do for them by simply using a series of words or phrases. From that I must pursue a dialogue that probes further, getting specific and throwing ideas back at them to see if I'm hearing what they're saying. They might use words like "tropical" or "clubby." They might mention a place like Provence or the Adirondacks. They might suggest a period of time like the 1940s. Those words are my starting point, my challenge.

It now becomes my job to interpret this message, these words, to distill these ideas and images. This is where we begin the next step: analyzing. What does all this mean?

"One has only to drift away into a dream to find inspiration."

—PAUL GAUGUIN

ANALYZE

Remember Peter Rogers's famous ad campaign for Black-glama—"What becomes a legend most?" A simple twist translates this concept to our homes. If we ask the question in relation to decorating, it turns into "What becomes our setting most?" I believe that if we assess our lifestyles realistically, then our decorating needs will come into sharper focus and we can solve many of our planning problems along the way.

After we've determined our general needs, we move on to home economics, otherwise known as the budget. Budget is usually the one element that restrains people from doing it all now, and from doing whatever it is they really want to do. But budget doesn't mean doing it on the cheap, it simply means establishing a financial plan and schedule that makes sense to you. In fact, I prefer to use the term "with a budget": it sounds more businesslike than "on a budget," which suggests shortcuts. The former is just a more positive approach to the process.

Nobody sets out to create a room that looks like a budget deficit. After all, working with a budget is what all smart people do. Regardless of how much money you have or don't have, budgeting and planning is the only sensible way to approach any decorating project. Once your room is decorated, it is there to stay and it should last for a very long time. You must look at, pass through, and sit in that room every day. In addition, analyzing is a mechanical process. It deals with the nuts and bolts of the room—the architecture, the traffic flow, lighting sources, and of course, the room's eventual use.

Forget color, forget fabrics, forget rugs and curtains, and forget about all those fabulous decorative items that you want. At this stage, focus only on the bare-bones mechanics of the room. For now you must trust me. Once you've laid out your plan in black and white, a plan that will really work for you, then and only then should you begin the process of decoration.

"Isn't practicality an aesthetic decision about life?"
—ETTORE SOTTSASS

First, you must measure the room as accurately as possible, noting the location of doors, windows, electrical outlets, fireplaces, steps, and so forth. If you are using existing furniture, each piece must be carefully measured. The height, depth, and width must be recorded. If I am shopping for a client or going to an antiques show, I always carry my measuring tape, my notes on measurements, and a list of pieces for which I'm shopping. Sometimes I take blueprints of the room.

This phase of the project also requires that you ask yourself a series of questions:

- How will each room be used?
- Who will use it the most?
- At what time of day will it mostly be used?
- What are the sources of light?
- Where are the windows and in which direction do they face?
- Location of doors will dictate a traffic pattern. How will this affect your desired furniture placement?
- Where are the electrical outlets and air-conditioning and heating units?

The floor plan, one element in the master plan, should determine the type and location of all furniture in a room. If you don't do a floor plan before buying furniture, you run the risk of buying the wrong sizes and ending up with a jumble of things, rather than having a room that exudes a peaceful harmony of furniture, accessories, and colors.

We all know people who have made mistakes, sometimes very costly ones. My advice is simply that you not overlook the

"The real act of discovery consists not in finding new lands but in new eyes."

—MARCEL PROUST

basics. Once you understand the importance of a master plan, your decorating project will be a lot easier.

VISUALIZE

Now let's move to the *decorating* phase, the visual part of the process. To begin, start by asking yourself another group of questions:

- Which colors do you prefer?
- What about textures and patterns?
- Light or dark?
- Muted colors or primary colors?
- What furniture do you have that you want to use in the room?
- What types of pieces does this room need to function?
- What other furniture types and styles do you see in this room?
- Have you been working around something that you're not in love with?
- Is your goal to create a formal, country, modern, or eclectic room?
- Are antiques to be included?
- Are you starting from scratch or using existing pieces?
- Have you tried to analyze all those magazine clippings you've been saving? What are they telling you?

I'm sure you will think of other questions. At this point in your planning, you must answer these specific questions to tie together the room that you fantasized with the physical aspects of the room you have. The answers to these questions

"Vision is the art of seeing things invisible."
—MRS. PERCY WYNDHAM

help you to visualize how to fit what you want into what you have.

OBSERVE

Observing and doing your homework constitute the next step in our process. In fact, smart shoppers are doing this all the time. Observing what's around you, shopping to see what's available, reading books and magazines, going to trade shows and decorator showhouses; all these things will inform you and influence your decisions. Keep an open mind and you'll discover more than you bargained for. You never know what will spark your imagination.

Some things that have acted as design catalysts for me include:

- a pattern from a Japanese fabric that was adapted and stenciled on a wall
- a particular English garden that inspired a mural
- the color of a robin's egg
- a fabulous Gothic book cabinet found at auction
- the color of a Tuscan farmhouse
- antique architectural elements that I had copied in fiber-glass, resin, and wood for urns, vases, and lamps
- patterns and designs from porcelain

and on and on.

Inspiration awaits us.

REALIZE

Very simply, this is the stage where we actually start to make

"Almost every interior of any grandeur in the history of interior decoration started out as someone's fantasy, realized by more or less theatrical means."

—STEPHEN CALLOWAY

concrete decisions based on fantasizing, analyzing, visualizing, and observing. We have now decided on style, color, layout, type of furniture, floor coverings, and how to treat our windows. We can now order, shop, paint, paper, hang pictures, and move the furniture in. We can turn on the lights, plump the cushions, find the right spot for each accessory, arrange the flowers, turn on the music, and settle in.

Fantasizing, Analyzing, Visualizing, Observing, and Realizing—do yourself a favor; the fun is in the process.

Color Palette

Raspberry

Champagne

Olive

Fabrics:

Striped moiré—walls

Raspberry velvet—chair cushions

Champagne linen—window treatments

Paint:

Off-white—trim and ceiling

A Formal Dining Room with a View to the Garden

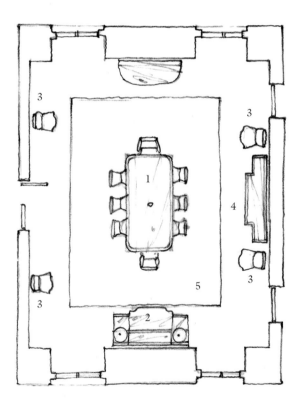

1. TWO-PEDESTAL MAHOGANY DINING ROOM TABLE
2. MAHOGANY SIDEBOARD 3. SET OF TWELVE
PAINTED REGENCY-STYLE DINING ROOM CHAIRS
4. MAHOGANY BREAKFRONT 5. ORIENTAL RUG

STAGE I

ALL THE ELEMENTS USED IN THIS ROOM WERE SELECTED TO IMPART AN OVERALL AIR OF ELEGANCE AND FORMALITY. THE ROOM IS A LARGE, RECTANGULAR SPACE WITH A HIGH CEILING. ARCHITECTURAL DETAILS INCLUDE A WIDE YET SIMPLE MOLDING AROUND THE PERIMETER AT THE CEILING LINE. TWO PAIRS OF FRENCH DOORS AT EACH END OF THE SPACE PROVIDE AMPLE LIGHT AS WELL AS INVITING VIEWS TO THE GARDEN. ONE PAIR FLANKS A LARGE MARBLE FIREPLACE (VISIBLE ONLY IN THE FLOOR PLAN); THE OTHER PAIR FLANKS THE MAHOGANY SIDEBOARD. A RAISED PANEL DADO ENCIRCLES THE ROOM. SLEEK BLACK REGENCY-STYLE CHAIRS ENHANCE THE ROOM'S REFINED ATMOSPHERE.

❧ THE EXISTING DOORS LEADING INTO THE ROOM ARE REPLACED WITH NEW ONES IN MAHOGANY TO ADD WEIGHT, IMPORTANCE, AND RICHNESS TO THE ENTRY, TO FURTHER DELINEATE THE MOLDING AROUND THEM, AND TO HARMONIZE WITH THE FURNITURE ALREADY IN THE ROOM.

❧ THE DINING ROOM BASICS, A TABLE AND CHAIRS, ARE CENTRALLY PLACED BELOW THE CHANDELIER AND ESTABLISH THE ROOM'S CIRCULATION PATTERN.

❧ THE FLOOR PLAN FOR THE ROOM SHOWS THE TABLE PLACED PERPENDICULAR TO THE ENTRANCE TO ALLOW FOR EASE OF MOVEMENT AND TO MAKE MAXIMUM USE OF THE SPACE.

STAGE II

THE ARCHITECTURAL ELEMENTS GUIDED THE SELECTION OF COLORS, FABRICS, AND FURNITURE, WITH THE PURPOSE OF CREATING A FORMAL AND ELEGANT SPACE IN A SUBTLE AND SOPHISTICATED COLOR SCHEME. THE UNUSUAL COLORS OF CHAMPAGNE, OLIVE, AND RASPBERRY FURTHER FORTIFY THE SUMPTUOUS TONE ESTABLISHED BY THE CLASSICAL ARCHITECTURE.

❧ THE ARCHITECTURAL ELEMENTS—THE DADO, THE CEILING MOLDING, AND THE CARVED PEDIMENT OVERDOOR—ARE PAINTED LINEN WHITE, WHICH LIGHTENS THE SPACE AND ADDS GENTLE CONTRAST TO THE STRIPED FABRIC OF THE WALLS.

❧ THE STRONG VERTICALITY OF THE STRIPED MOIRÉ WALLS REINFORCES THE HEIGHT OF THE ROOM.

❧ A LARGE AND DARK FLORAL PAINTING IS HUNG OVER THE SIDEBOARD AND A LIDDED URN IS PLACED ON EACH SIDE.

❧ RASPBERRY VELVET IS USED ON THE DINING ROOM CHAIR CUSHIONS, WHICH HAVE A MULTICOLORED ROPE IN A CRISS-CROSS PATTERN CONNECTING SMALL BUTTON TUFTS.

"The rooms that are really successful declare the owner's independence, and carry the owner's signature, his very private scrawl." —BILLY BALDWIN

STAGE III

T HE FINISHING TOUCHES ARE ADDED IN THIS FINAL STAGE OF DECORATION, WITH AN EYE TOWARD KEEPING THE ROOM SIMPLE AND AVOIDING DECORATIVE OVERKILL.

⚜ AN ANTIQUE ORIENTAL AREA RUG IS PLACED UNDER THE TABLE TO ANCHOR THE SPACE AND TO SOFTEN THE HARD PLANES OF THE ROOM.

⚜ A PLANTER FILLED WITH LARGE, WHITE, FRAGRANT BLOSSOMS OF MAGNOLIA IS PLACED ON TOP OF THE SIDEBOARD TO FILL THE LARGE AREA BETWEEN THE URNS AND TO GIVE A WARM WELCOME.

⚜ A LARGE LIDDED IRONSTONE TUREEN PLAYS THE ROLE OF PERMANENT CENTERPIECE ON THE DINING ROOM TABLE. FOR VARIETY, IT COULD BE FILLED WITH FLOWERS OR FRUIT.

⚜ AS AN ALTERNATIVE TO THE FLORAL PAINTING IN STAGE II, A LIGHT LANDSCAPE IS USED HERE TO CREATE A DIFFERENT FEELING IN THE ROOM.

⚜ A SUBTLE TONE-ON-TONE CHAMPAGNE-COLORED DAMASK IS USED IN THE WINDOW TREATMENTS. ITS SCALLOPED VALANCE AND JABOT ARE GIVEN VISUAL PUNCH BY THE SILK FRINGE IN OLIVE AND RASPBERRY.

Variations

*T*WO PAIRS OF CANDLESTICKS PLACED STRICTLY IN A ROW AND SURROUNDED SYMMETRICALLY BY SIX SMALL VASES CAN BE USED FOR A FORMAL DINNER AS WELL AS AN AFTERNOON TEA. FOR A MORE RELAXED APPROACH, THE SAME LILY-OF-THE-VALLEY SPRIGS COULD BE PLACED IN ODD VASES, WITH UNMATCHED CANDLESTICKS, IN A LESS SYMMETRICAL FORMATION.

A PAIR OF TALL SILVER CANDELABRA FLANK A FOOTED SILVER TUREEN OVERFLOWING WITH LARGE OPEN ROSES. THIS CENTERPIECE IDEA IS APPROPRIATE FOR A FORMAL DINNER OR AN ELEGANT BUFFET. THE SAME TUREEN FILLED WITH COLORFUL GARDEN ZINNIAS AND OFFSET BY BEESWAX CANDLES IN SIMPLE GLASS HOLDERS WOULD BE GREAT FOR A RELAXED SUMMERTIME DINNER.

You can create various moods and themes easily in this room by changing the items and their location on the dining table. In a formal dining room like this one, relaxation of the room can be achieved by changing the centerpiece container, the way in which the table is set, and the flowers (or fruits) chosen.

THIS GATHERING OF DAFFODILS POTTED IN SIMPLE TERRA-COTTA GARDEN POTS AMID VOTIVE CANDLES IN SMALLER POTS IS SUITABLE FOR A SUNDAY BRUNCH OR A SPRINGTIME LUNCHEON OR DINNER. WHEN THESE ITEMS ARE PLACED IN AN UNSTRUCTURED, ASYMMETRICAL ARRANGEMENT AT THE CENTER OF THE TABLE, THE ATMOSPHERE IS RELAXED EVEN FURTHER.

A FOOTED BOWL FILLED WITH A VARIETY OF FRUITS AND FLOWERS IS PLACED AMID SIX VOTIVE CANDLES WRAPPED IN GALAX LEAVES AND TIED WITH RAFFIA. THIS ABUNDANT CENTERPIECE IS A THOUGHTFUL CHOICE FOR ANY DINNER PARTY. YOU MIGHT TRY FILLING THE BOWL WITH LEMONS, LIMES, AND MORE GALAX LEAVES FOR A SUMMERY, TROPICAL THEME.

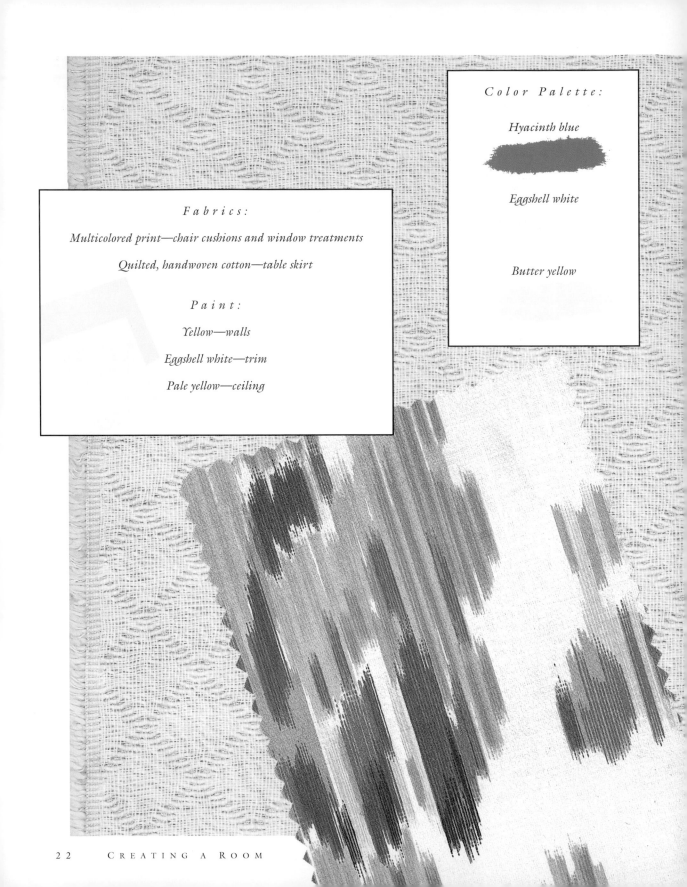

Color Palette:

Hyacinth blue

Eggshell white

Butter yellow

Fabrics:

Multicolored print—chair cushions and window treatments

Quilted, handwoven cotton—table skirt

Paint:

Yellow—walls

Eggshell white—trim

Pale yellow—ceiling

An Intimate Dining Room with a Swedish Accent

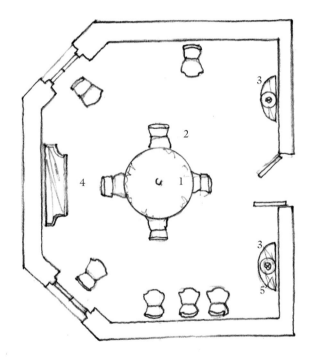

1. ROUND DINING ROOM TABLE 2. SET OF TEN DINING
ROOM CHAIRS 3. PAIR OF PAINTED DEMI-LUNE
CABINETS 4. PAINTED CONSOLE/BUFFET TABLE
5. PAIR OF URN-SHAPED LAMPS ON EACH CABINET

STAGE I

A DINING ROOM WAS CREATED OUT OF THIS SMALL SIX-SIDED SPACE FILLED WITH ANGLES AND CORNERS. THE MOST LOGICAL PLACE FOR THE ROUND DINING ROOM TABLE IS DEAD CENTER IN THE ROOM, ALLOWING FOR THE MOST EFFICIENT USE OF SPACE. THE EXTRA CHAIRS ARE PLACED AROUND THE ROOM TO KEEP THE TABLE FROM APPEARING CRAMPED. A CONSOLE TABLE AND TWO DEMI-LUNE CABINETS (VISIBLE ONLY IN THE FLOOR PLAN) FLANKING THE ENTRANCE ADD WEIGHT AND BALANCE TO THE ROOM. A PAIR OF URN-SHAPED LAMPS ON THE DEMI-LUNE CABINETS PROVIDE LIGHT TO THIS SIDE OF THE ROOM.

⁜ THE CIRCULAR TABLE WAS CHOSEN TO ENCOURAGE INTIMATE GATHER-INGS AND TO HIGHLIGHT THE ROOM'S UNIQUE HEXAGONAL SHAPE.

⁜ THE CHANDELIER PROVIDES ARTIFICIAL LIGHT TO THE MAIN AREA OF THE ROOM.

⁜ THE ARCHITECTURAL DETAILS, WHICH ACCENTUATE THE HEXAGONAL SHAPE OF THE ROOM, INCLUDE MOLDING AT THE CEILING LINE AND BASE-BOARD AND A CHAIR RAIL.

⁜ A TABLE SKIRT WAS ADDED AT THIS STAGE, AS THE TABLE UNDERNEATH IS QUITE PLAIN. THE SKIRT PROVIDES FULLNESS TO A ROOM THAT MIGHT OTHERWISE APPEAR LEGGY.

⁜ THE FLOOR IS COVERED WITH A RUG WOVEN GEOMETRICALLY OF SISAL, A PRACTICAL, DURABLE, AND WIDELY AVAILABLE MATERIAL.

Jim Steinmeyer 1993

STAGE II

IN THE SECOND STAGE, THIS SMALL DINING AREA IS BRIGHTENED BY PAINTING THE WALLS A SOFT BUTTER YELLOW THAT NATURALLY WARMS THE ROOM AS IF BY SUNLIGHT. EGGSHELL WHITE IS USED ON THE MOLDING SURROUNDING THE PERIMETER AT THE CEILING LINE. THE WALL BELOW THE CHAIR RAIL IS PAINTED THE SAME COLOR AS THE MOLDING TO CREATE A SENSE OF BALANCE. A FAUX-MARBLE PAINTING TECHNIQUE IS USED ON THE BASEBOARD, WHICH DEFINES THE "ODD" SHAPE OF THE ROOM, ANCHORS THE LIGHT-COLORED WALLS, AND ADDS VISUAL INTEREST IN THIS SMALL ROOM.

❧ THE COLOR PALETTE SELECTED FOR THIS DINING ROOM IS SOFT AND WARM. THE HYACINTH-AND-WHITE PRINT FABRIC ON THE CHAIR SEATS, WITH TOUCHES OF ROSE, FORTIFIES THE BUTTER-YELLOW WALLS AND EGGSHELL-WHITE MOLDINGS.

❧ ALL THE NINETEENTH-CENTURY SWEDISH-STYLE FURNITURE IN THIS ROOM IS PAINTED IN SHADES OF WHITE WITH A GENTLE WASH OF GRAY, AS IS CUSTOMARY FOR FURNITURE FROM THIS PERIOD.

❧ FLORAL WATERCOLORS ARE HUNG ON THE WALL TO THE RIGHT OF THE CONSOLE AND THE FRENCH DOORS TO BRING ATTENTION TO YET ANOTHER ANGLE OF THE ROOM'S ODD SHAPE AND TO REFLECT THE GARDEN JUST BEYOND THE DOORS.

"The best ornament for a dining room is a well cooked dinner." —MRS. HAWEIS

STAGE III

T HE SIMPLE FLOOR COVERING, BRIGHT COLORS, AND LIGHTLY PAINTED FURNITURE NOW IN PLACE ARE ADDED TO IN THE LAST STAGE TO ESTABLISH A DISTINCTIVE AND LIGHT DINING ROOM WITH A SWEDISH ACCENT. THE VARIETY OF DECORATIVE TOUCHES INTRODUCED HERE ENSURES THAT, EVEN ON THE GLOOMIEST DAYS, THIS CHEERFUL ROOM WILL OFFER A SPOT OF COMFORT AND TRANQUILLITY.

⚜ THE ASYMMETRICAL SWAGS DRAPED OVER HEAVY WOODEN RODS WITH GILDED FINIALS SOFTEN THE LARGE AMOUNT OF GLASS IN THE ROOM. AN EGGSHELL-COLORED BULLION FRINGE ADDS A FINISHING TOUCH AND HELPS DEFINE THE DRAPE OF THE FABRIC. REPEATING FABRICS, AND IN THIS CASE USING ONLY TWO FABRICS, PROVIDES BALANCE AND A UNIFYING QUALITY THAT MAKES A ROOM CLEAN AND SIMPLE.

⚜ A LARGE, GILT-FRAMED FRENCH PASTORAL PAINTING IS CENTERED ABOVE THE LIGHTLY PAINTED CONSOLE.

⚜ A MARBLE BUST OF AN EIGHTEENTH-CENTURY LADY IS BALANCED BY TWO PAIRS OF CREAMWARE CACHEPOTS. THE LARGER PAIR HAS BEEN POTTED WITH HYDRANGEA; THE SMALLER PAIR IS FILLED WITH COLORFUL GRAPE HYACINTH.

⚜ A COLLECTION OF LARGE BLUE-AND-WHITE PORCELAIN JARS ADDS A DASH OF COLOR AND PATTERN, WHILE SIMULTANEOUSLY PROVIDING VOLUME AND MASS IN WHAT WOULD HAVE BEEN AN EMPTY SPACE UNDERNEATH THE CONSOLE—AN UNUSUAL BUT EFFECTIVE LOCATION FOR THESE LARGE JARS.

⚜ THE CENTERPIECE ON THE DINING ROOM TABLE IS AN OPENWORK CREAMWARE BOWL ABUNDANTLY FILLED WITH LEMONS.

⚜ AN OVAL PICTURE HAS BEEN ADDED ABOVE THE EXISTING WATERCOLOR, WHICH VISUALLY BALANCES THE HEIGHT OF THE PAINTING ON THE ADJACENT WALL.

Variations

A MORE OPULENT LOOK IS PRODUCED BY HANG-
ING TWO CURTAIN PANELS ON ONE PAINTED
WOODEN ROD WITH FINIALS. THE BOTTOM PANEL
IS A SOLID EGGSHELL-COLORED FABRIC, TRIMMED
IN A BLUE-AND-WHITE STRIPE AND CUT ON THE
BIAS. THE TOP PANEL IS A VERTICAL BLUE-AND-
WHITE STRIPE WITH THE SAME TRIM, ALSO CUT ON
THE BIAS. THIS TOP PANEL IS HAND-TIED TO THE
ROD WITH TABS. BOTH DRAPES ARE GATHERED
AND HELD TO THE SIDE BY A TIEBACK SUPPORTED
BY A LARGE BRASS MEDALLION. A BLUE-AND-WHITE
CHECKED FABRIC ON THE CHAIR SEAT COMPLE-
MENTS THE STRIPE IN THE DRAPE.

A SOLID HYACINTH-BLUE SILK DRAPE IS TOPPED
WITH A SOFT VALANCE, SHAPED BY A ZIGZAG HEM.
A STRAIGHT VALANCE OF THIS TYPE UTILIZES THE
LEAST AMOUNT OF FABRIC BUT SACRIFICES NOTH-
ING IN STYLE. EACH POINT IS FINISHED WITH A SILK
TASSEL IN BLUE AND EGGSHELL. A PAINTED
SWEDISH PLANT STAND PLACED DIRECTLY IN FRONT
OF THE WINDOW IS FILLED WITH ASSORTED FRA-
GRANT HERBAL TOPIARIES AT VARIOUS HEIGHTS,
UNDERPLANTED WITH IVY.

Due to the size of the room, two of the key components to the room's design are the windows and the wall that separates them. Therefore, two options for both the window treatments and the wall with the sideboard are illustrated here.

The graceful console has been replaced with a painted nineteenth-century-style chest. Vintage cream-colored porcelain is symmetrically arranged above the chest, and an elaborate pair of crystal candlesticks sit alongside a simple wooden flat of yellow parrot tulips. In a small dining room, a chest can provide a place to store linens and silver. At the same time, if the dining room table were not skirted, the chest would provide mass to an otherwise leggy room.

The French pastoral painting has been replaced by a painted Swedish mirror. Mirrors can add a romantic quality to a room—a dining room, particularly—because they reflect the flicker of candlelight from the table and lighting above. A pair of glass candlestick lamps, topped with shades that have diagonally gathered fabric, sit at either end of the console. A cut-glass footed bowl in the center overflows with white parrot tulips. Since you could not have a centerpiece this high in the middle of the dining table, because your guests would never be able to see one another, the console is the place to do something on a larger scale. A large natural sea grass basket filled with birch logs sits underneath the console to serve the fireplace in the small adjacent living room, constantly used during the winter months.

Color Palette:

Tomato

Delft

Ocher

Ivory

Fabrics:

Tomato damask—sofa, window shades

Ivory solid textured cotton—slipper chairs

Striped damask—table skirt

Paint:

Ocher—walls

Ivory—trim and ceiling

A Warm Sitting Room/Library

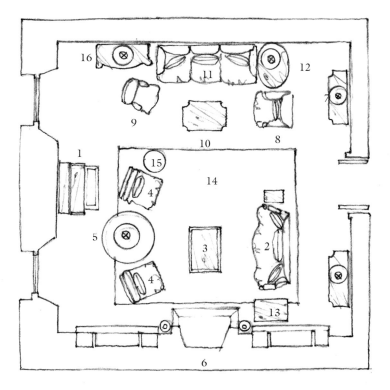

1. SLANT-FRONT DESK 2. FRENCH SOFA 3. LARGE COFFEE TABLE
4. PAIR OF ARMLESS UPHOLSTERED CHAIRS 5. ROUND DRAPED TABLE
6. GILT MIRROR 7. PAIR OF OVERSCALED THREE-TIER BOOK TABLES
8. LARGE CLUB CHAIR 9. SMALL CLUB CHAIR
10. FRENCH UPHOLSTERED OTTOMAN 11. SOFA 12. OVAL MAHOGANY
SIDE TABLE 13. SMALL MAHOGANY TEA TABLE 14. ORIENTAL RUG
15. CERAMIC GARDEN SEAT 16. PEMBROKE TABLE

STAGE I

THE FURNITURE IN THIS ROOM IS ASSEMBLED INTO TWO DISTINCT SEATING AREAS. THE MOST IMPORTANT AREA, CONTAINING THE CARVED FRENCH SOFA, IS CLUSTERED PERPENDICULAR TO THE FIREPLACE. THE OTHER AREA IS LOCATED AGAINST THE EXPANSE OF WALL OPPOSITE THE FIREPLACE. THIS SUBTLE DIVISION PROVIDES TWO INTIMATE SPACES FOR READING OR FOR ENTERTAINING A LARGER GROUP. EACH CHAIR AND SOFA HAS A TABLE CONVENIENTLY PLACED NEAR IT FOR HOLDING A DRINK OR A MAGAZINE "IN PROGRESS." THE BOOK TABLES FLANKING THE DOOR (VISIBLE ONLY IN THE FLOOR PLAN) ALLOW FOR THE OVERFLOW OF BOOKS AND THE MONTHLY COLLECTION OF MAGAZINES. A PAIR OF ELONGATED, DEEP-SET WINDOWS ARE FRAMED WITH WOODEN PANELS. ACROSS FROM THE SOFA, TWO ARMLESS SLIPPER CHAIRS ARE PLACED ON EITHER SIDE OF A ROUND SKIRTED TABLE.

❀ AN OVERSIZED FRENCH COFFEE TABLE IS CENTERED ON THE AREA RUG.

❀ THE ROOM IS A LARGE, SQUARE SPACE, WITH A HIGH CEILING. ARCHITECTURAL DETAILS INCLUDE BASEBOARDS, A CHAIR RAIL, AND A HEAVY CROWN MOLDING AROUND THE PERIMETER AT THE CEILING LINE.

❀ THE SMALL REPEAT OF THE WALL-TO-WALL CARPET PATTERN ADDS OVERALL WARMTH. AN ORIENTAL RUG HAS BEEN PLACED ON TOP OF THE CARPETING TO FURTHER DEFINE THE PRIMARY SEATING AREA.

❀ THE DARK MAHOGANY SLANT-FRONT DESK ADDS WEIGHT—AND THEREFORE BALANCE—TO THE SPACE BETWEEN THE TWO LARGE PAINTED PANELED WINDOWS.

STAGE II

THE COLORS INTRODUCED IN STAGE II ARE WARM, RICH, AND LIGHT, PERFECT FOR AN INTIMATE ROOM WITH SUCH STRONG ARCHITECTURAL DETAIL. THE WALLS ABOVE THE CHAIR RAIL ARE PAINTED OCHER. THE CEILING, MOLDINGS, BOOKCASES, AND LOWER PORTION OF THE WALL ARE PAINTED IVORY.

❧ A LARGE GILT BROKEN-PEDIMENT MIRROR HANGS ABOVE THE FIREPLACE, ENHANCING THE FOCAL POINT OF THE ROOM. THIS TYPE OF MIRROR EMPHASIZES THE OTHER DETAILS AND AT THE SAME TIME ADDS MORE "ARCHITECTURE" TO THE ROOM.

❧ LIGHTING IS SUBDUED, PROVIDED BY THE SWING-ARM BRASS LAMPS BESIDE THE FIREPLACE WITH THEIR GATHERED IVORY SILK SHADES. SWING-ARM LAMPS ATTACHED TO THE WALL IN THIS MANNER ELIMINATE THE NEED FOR A TABLE AND LAMP, WHICH WOULD, IN THIS CASE, INHIBIT TRAFFIC FLOW INTO THIS CORNER OF THE ROOM.

❧ ADDITIONAL DASHES OF COLOR AND TEXTURE ARE PROVIDED BY THE PLUMP AUBUSSON PILLOWS PLACED ON THE SOFA.

❧ TWO PAINTINGS ADDED ABOVE THE DESK BALANCE THE VERTICALITY OF THE FIREPLACE WALL. A LIDDED WOODEN BOX ATOP THE DESK FILLS THE SPACE BETWEEN THE PAINTINGS AND DESK TOP AND MAY HOLD STATIONERY OR OTHER PAPERWORK.

❧ BOOKS, A FEW SELECT PORCELAINS, AND A PLANT ON THE COFFEE TABLE BEGIN TO TELL A STORY.

❧ THE ROUND SKIRTED TABLE HAS BEEN TOPPED BY A FAMILY PHOTO, CURRENT BOOKS, AND A STRIPED TOLE CACHEPOT.

STAGE III

ANY OF THE OBJECTS ADDED AT THIS STAGE ARE IN BLUE AND WHITE TO INFUSE THE ROOM WITH A UNIFYING ACCENT COLOR. BLUE AND WHITE PROVIDE A CRISP CONTRAST TO THE OCHER AND IVORY ON THE WALLS WHILE TYING IN WITH THE BLUE IN BOTH THE WALL-TO-WALL AND ORIENTAL CARPETS. WHILE THIS PARTICULAR COORDINATION OF COLOR IS NOT ESSENTIAL TO BRING THIS ROOM TOGETHER, IT NEVERTHELESS MAKES A STRONG STATEMENT. BLUE AND WHITE IS A COLOR COMBINATION THAT MOST PEOPLE FIND VERY APPEALING, PRIMARILY BECAUSE OF ITS CLEAN APPEARANCE.

❀ MORE BLUE-AND-WHITE PORCELAINS ARE ADDED—TO THE BOOKCASES, MANTEL, AND SLANT-FRONT DESK.

❀ A PORCELAIN GARDEN SEAT SERVES AS AN END TABLE.

❀ ONE JAR ON A BRACKET RAISES THE EYE EVEN FARTHER AND ADDS A NEW DIMENSION TO THIS WALL.

❀ A LARGE PORCELAIN GINGER-JAR LAMP, PLACED ON THE SKIRTED TABLE, ALSO HAS A GATHERED IVORY SILK SHADE TO ALLOW FOR MAXIMUM LIGHT BETWEEN THE TWO CHAIRS.

❀ PAINTINGS OF LANDSCAPES CONSTITUTE THE MAJORITY OF THE ARTWORK.

❀ THE FABRIC USED ON THE SOFA IS ALSO USED FOR THE WINDOW SHADES. USING THE SAME FABRIC AND COLOR ON BOTH SIDES OF THE ROOM HELPS TO BALANCE THE OVERALL SCHEME.

❀ EACH ARMLESS SLIPPER CHAIR NOW HOLDS AN AUBUSSON TAPESTRY PILLOW, SIMILAR TO THOSE ON THE COUCH.

❀ ADDITIONAL PLANTS, PLATES, BOXES, PICTURES, AND BOOKS ARE PLACED THROUGHOUT, AS EVIDENCE THAT THIS ROOM IS USED FREQUENTLY AS AN INTIMATE GATHERING SPOT.

❀ THE CANDLESTICKS ON THE COFFEE TABLE, WHEN LIT, WOULD HEIGHTEN THE COZINESS OF THE SEATING AREA.

"*More than anything else, I love the possessions people have either inherited or are going to hand down, for it is these that give a room a personal character.*"—ROSE CUMMING

Variations

A LARGE ARMOIRE SUPPORTS A COLLECTION OF BLUE-AND-WHITE PORCELAIN, CLUSTERED TO DELIVER MAXIMUM IMPACT. EVEN THOUGH THE ARMOIRE IS A MASSIVE PIECE, THE SCALE OF THE ROOM CAN COMFORTABLY ACCOMMODATE IT. A PIECE THIS SIZE COULD EASILY OVERWHELM A SMALLER SPACE WITH LOWER CEILINGS.

A SIMPLE FRUITWOOD CHEST—TOPPED BY A GILT-WOOD-BASED PORCELAIN LAMP WITH A FRINGED SILK SHADE AND A FEW PERSONAL OBJECTS—CREATES AN INVITING AND WARM TABLEAU. BOOKS, PHOTOGRAPHS, AND A LIDDED URN ARE THE OBJECTS OF CHOICE. A CHEST OF SUCH SMALL SCALE WARRANTS THE USE OF ONLY ONE LAMP THIS SIZE. A LARGE, OVAL GILT-FRAMED MIRROR HUNG BY A SILK ROPE WITH TASSELS PROVIDES ADDED DETAIL. THE ROPE DRAWS THE EYE TO ABOVE THE TOP OF THE MIRROR AND EMPHASIZES THE CEILING HEIGHT.

A wall between two windows can be treated any number of ways. In this case, because of the ceiling height, vertical treatments work best in keeping a balance in scale and mass.

A GILT-FRAMED PAINTING RESTS ABOVE AN ELABORATE CONSOLE WITH BRASS INLAY AND TWO HAND-CARVED DOLPHINS ON ITS BASE. BECAUSE OF THE FORMAL NATURE OF THE CONSOLE, THE PAINTING ABOVE HAS BEEN FRAMED IN GOLD. A MIXED GROUP OF BLUE-AND-WHITE PORCELAIN IS DISPLAYED ON TOP IN A RANDOM ORDER. THE SMALLER SCALE OF THIS CONSOLE TABLE WARRANTS THE USE OF ONLY ONE LAMP, WHICH THROWS A WELCOME NOTE OF ASYMMETRY INTO THIS OTHER-WISE SYMMETRICALLY BALANCED ROOM.

A LARGE UNFRAMED OIL CENTERED ABOVE A CLEAN-LINED WALNUT CONSOLE ADDS A CASUAL NOTE TO A ROOM THAT COULD OTHERWISE BE VIEWED AS GRAND. A PAIR OF TWISTED MARBLE LAMPS, CROWNED WITH TOMATO-RED SILK COOLIE SHADES, ARE PLACED ON EITHER SIDE OF A BLUE-AND-WHITE PORCELAIN CACHEPOT FILLED WITH WHITE CAMELLIAS. THE RED SHADES EMPHASIZE ONE COMPONENT OF THE COLOR SCHEME, WHILE THE BLUE-AND-WHITE PORCELAIN CONTINUES THE THEME OF THE ROOM'S KEY ACCESSORIES. THIS VARIATION REPRESENTS A SIMPLE, UNCLUTTERED APPROACH.

Fabrics:

Floral—sofa and ottoman

Green velvet—side chair

Plaid moiré—slipper chairs

Small green check—table skirt

Pink check—throw pillow on sofa

Paint:

Periwinkle—walls

China white—trim and ceiling

Color Palette:

Periwinkle

Magnolia

Rose

Aqua

Grass

A Colorful Room for Living

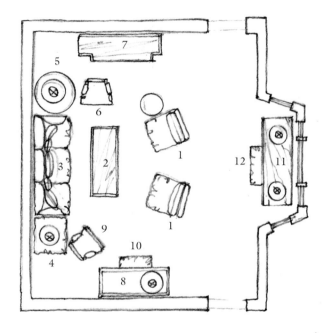

1. PAIR OF ARMLESS SLIPPER CHAIRS 2. TWO-TIERED
PAINTED RECTANGULAR COFFEE TABLE 3. SOFA
4. DRAPED SOFA TABLE 5. ROUND FRUITWOOD SIDE
TABLE 6. SMALL UPHOLSTERED ARMCHAIR
7. ARMOIRE CONTAINING TV AND STEREO
8. PAINTED CONSOLE TABLE 9. PAINTED ARMCHAIR
10. UPHOLSTERED FLORAL OTTOMAN
11. LARGE FRUITWOOD DESK 12. DESK CHAIR

STAGE I

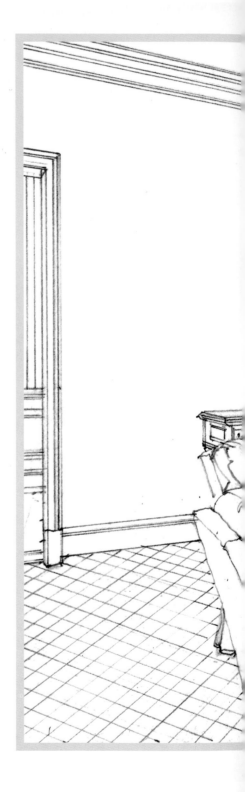

T HE UPHOLSTERED FURNITURE IN THIS SQUARE ROOM IS CLUSTERED TO ONE SIDE TO CREATE A COZY, CONVERSATIONAL GROUPING. THE ARRANGEMENT ALSO LEAVES A CLEAR PATH BETWEEN THE TWO ENTRANCES TO THE ROOM TO ALLOW FOR EASE OF MOVEMENT FROM THE FOYER TO THE MAIN HALLWAY DOWNSTAIRS. A LARGE ARMOIRE (VISI-BLE ONLY IN THE FLOOR PLAN) ACROSS FROM THE CONSOLE WALL HOUSES AND SIMULTANEOUSLY DISGUISES A TELEVISION AND STEREO SYSTEM. THE RELATIVELY LOW CEILING IS PAINTED WHITE TO MAKE IT APPEAR HIGHER AND TO REFLECT THE COLORS BELOW. SIMPLE MOLDINGS ARE ALSO PAINTED WHITE, TO BLEND WITH THE CEILING LINE AND TO REIN-FORCE THE OVERALL THEME OF CRISPNESS AND SIMPLICITY. THE FURNISHINGS ARE SIMPLE YET NOT PLAIN.

❧ THE GEOMETRIC PATTERN OF THE WALL-TO-WALL CARPETING CRE-ATES A COZY FEELING AND LINKS ALL THE FURNISHINGS BY REPEATING THE GARDEN TONES THAT ARE THEMATIC IN THIS ROOM.

❧ A SMALL UPHOLSTERED ARMCHAIR STANDS TO THE RIGHT OF THE SOFA.

❧ ADDITIONAL SEATING IS PROVIDED BY A PAIR OF ARMLESS UPHOL-STERED CHAIRS AND A PAINTED ARMCHAIR ANGLED IN THE CORNER WITH ACCESS TO BOTH THE SOFA AND THE CHAIRS.

S T A G E I I

IBRANT COLOR IS THE MAIN ELEMENT USED IN THIS COMFORTABLE AND INFORMAL LIVING ROOM. TONES OF MAGNOLIA, GRASS, ROSE, AND PERIWINKLE PREDOMINATE IN VARIOUS CHECKS, PLAIDS, AND FLORALS AND ESTABLISH VISUAL INTEREST WHERE SINGLE ARCHITECTURAL DETAILS ARE NOT A DOMINANT FEATURE.

❧ PAINTINGS ARE ADDED TO THE WALLS, AND LIGHTING, BOOKS, AND SEVERAL DECORATIVE OBJECTS ARE ADDED TO BOTH TIERS OF THE COFFEE TABLE AND TO THE CONSOLE.

❧ THE WALLS ARE PAINTED A VIVID SHADE OF PERIWINKLE.

❧ A PILLOW IN A SMALL ROSE CHECK COMPLEMENTS THE FLORAL FABRIC OF THE SOFA.

STAGE III

A GARDENLIKE FEELING IS FINALLY CREATED IN THIS COLORFUL AND REFRESHING LIVING ROOM. CLICHÉS ARE AVOIDED BY KNOWING HOW MUCH IS ENOUGH, AN INSTINCT THAT COMES FROM PRACTICE AND CAREFUL EDITING.

❧ ADDITIONAL ARTWORK, ACCESSORIES, FLOWERS, PLANTS, AND MORE BOOKS COMPLETE THE ROOM AND ADD TO ITS LIVED-IN FEELING.

❧ AN OTTOMAN, COVERED IN THE SAME FLORAL AS THE SOFA, IS COMFORTABLY STORED UNDERNEATH THE CONSOLE AND IS AVAILABLE SHOULD EXTRA SEATING BE REQUIRED.

❧ A PATTERNED PORCELAIN GARDEN SEAT USED AS A SIDE TABLE PROVIDES AN EFFECTIVE AND PRACTICAL PLACE TO SET A DRINK.

❧ THE HAND-PAINTED BOTANICAL PILLOWS ON THE SOFA REITERATE THIS GARDEN THEME, AS EACH REPRESENTS THE OWNER'S FAVORITE FLOWERS.

"*The room is most successful that seems to have happened spontaneously.*" —RUSSELL LYNES

Variations

A PAIR OF WOODEN CANDLESTICK LAMPS WITH PARCHMENT SHADES FLANK A VASE OF POPPIES AND A PICTURE ON AN EASEL. A LARGE MIRROR WITH A WOODEN PAINTED FRAME HOLDS A FEW SNAPSHOTS AND POSTCARDS RANDOMLY STUCK IN THE FRAME, GIVING THE ROOM A VERY PERSONAL FEELING.

A BRASS CANDLESTICK LAMP WITH A FRINGED SHADE IS BALANCED BY A TALL ARRANGEMENT OF LILACS. A SWEDISH CLOCK AND MINIATURE PAINTED LANDSCAPE FILL THE SPACE BETWEEN. FOR A MORE RELAXED LOOK, THE PAINTING RESTS ON TOP OF THE CONSOLE AND IS PLACED OFF CENTER BEHIND THE LAMP.

A console such as the one featured in this room is the perfect backdrop piece for spontaneous, fresh arrangements, future additions, and perpetual editing.

A FOOTED BASALT PLANTER BETWEEN TWO FIGURAL LAMPS RESTS BENEATH A FORMAL PORTRAIT. AS LAMPS IN THIS AREA OF THE ROOM ARE FOR GENERAL ILLUMINATION, AS OPPOSED TO TASK LIGHT—FOR READING AND SO ON—THEY CAN BE FITTED WITH LAMPSHADES MADE OF DARKER OR OPAQUE MATERIALS. THIS IS AN OPPORTUNITY TO BREAK THE MONOTONY OF USING ALL-WHITE LAMPSHADES.

A PILE OF FAVORITE BOOKS AND A BASKET OF POSTCARDS AND STATIONERY STAND READY FOR USE. AN URN FILLED WITH GLORIOUS MAGNOLIAS BRINGS FRAGRANCE INTO THE ROOM. AN UNUSUAL, EYE-CATCHING GOLD SUNBURST CLOCK MIRROR BRINGS DRAMA, WEIGHT, AND HEIGHT TO THIS WALL. THE ELABORATE NATURE OF THE CLOCK MIRROR NEEDS NO COMPETITION FROM A BUSY SURFACE BELOW; THEREFORE, ONLY A FEW ITEMS HAVE BEEN PLACED ON THE CONSOLE.

Fabrics:

Chintz—window treatments, love seat

Brown velvet—pair of channel-back chairs, banquettes

Woven coral—récamier

Linen print—trefoil and footstool

Small check—récamier bolster

Paint:

Beige and flat beige – trim and ceiling

Color Palette:

Beige

Coral

Chocolate

A Sunny and Sophisticated Living Room

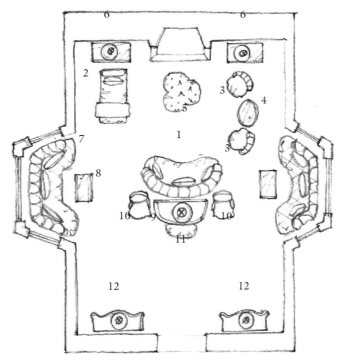

1. KIDNEY-SHAPED LOVE SEAT 2. RÉCAMIER
3. PAIR OF UPHOLSTERED CHANNEL-BACK CHAIRS
4. SIDE TABLE WITH LYRE-SHAPED BASE
5. TREFOIL-SHAPED OTTOMAN 6. PAIR OF CABINETS
7. PAIR OF UPHOLSTERED BANQUETTES 8. COFFEE TABLES
9. DEMI-LUNE CONSOLE 10. PAIR OF FRENCH ARMCHAIRS
11. FOOTSTOOL 12. PAIR OF TALL BOOKCASE CABINETS
TOPPED WITH BUSTS

S T A G E   I

L ARGE FORMAL LIVING ROOMS, WITH A PLETHORA OF ARCHITEC-
TURAL DETAILS, CAN BE A DAUNTING DESIGN CHALLENGE. TO
CREATE AN ELEGANT AND INTIMATE SPACE, YET AVOID A "HOTEL LOBBY"
AMBIENCE, IS NO EASY FEAT.

THE MAJORITY OF THE FURNITURE IN THIS LARGE ROOM IS CLUS-
TERED IN THE VICINITY OF THE FIREPLACE. TWO SYMMETRICAL BOW WIN-
DOWS ARE FITTED WITH CURVED, UPHOLSTERED BANQUETTES. LOCATING
THE SOFA IN THE MIDDLE OF THIS LARGE ROOM SERVES TO DEFINE, OR
ENCLOSE, A PORTION OF THE ROOM, MAKING IT MORE INTIMATE. THE
ENTRANCE TO THE ROOM IS FLANKED BY A PAIR OF TALL BOOKCASE CABI-
NETS (VISIBLE ONLY IN THE FLOOR PLAN). THESE CABINETS ADD WEIGHT
TO THIS END OF THE ROOM AS WELL AS AN ADDED DIMENSION OF HEIGHT.

⚜ THE PATTERNED WALL-TO-WALL CARPETING FILLS THE EXCEEDINGLY LARGE SPACE
WITH COLOR AND FOOLS THE EYE, MAKING THE ROOM APPEAR SMALLER AND LESS
FORBIDDING.

⚜ A LARGE RÉCAMIER FACES A LOVE SEAT.

⚜ A PAIR OF GRILLE-FRONT CABINETS SIT ASTRIDE THE FIREPLACE, WITH A TREFOIL
OTTOMAN IN FRONT.

⚜ A ROUND ROSEWOOD TABLE WITH A LYRE-SHAPED BASE IS POSITIONED BETWEEN
THE CHANNEL-BACK CHAIRS.

⚜ PLACED BEHIND THE LOVE SEAT IS A DEMI-LUNE CONSOLE FLANKED BY A PAIR OF
FRENCH UPHOLSTERED ARMCHAIRS. THIS ARRANGEMENT ANCHORS THE CENTER OF
THE ROOM IN A WAY THAT A SOFA ALONE CANNOT.

⚜ A LANTERN HUNG ABOVE THIS GROUPING PROVIDES THE ONLY SOURCE OF OVER-
HEAD LIGHT IN THE ROOM.

STAGE II

T O MAKE THIS SPACE APPROACHABLE AND AT THE SAME TIME MAINTAIN ITS STATURE, WITH-OUT ESTABLISHING A STUFFY ATMOSPHERE, NATURAL COLORS AND SUBTLE YET DIVERSIFIED TEXTURES WERE SELECTED. A BEIGE DAMASK-DESIGN WALLPAPER IN-TRODUCES SUBDUED PATTERN TO THE ROOM AND MOVEMENT TO THE WALLS.

❋ THE PANELING AND MOLDINGS ARE PAINTED A LIGHTER SHADE OF BEIGE TO MAKE THEM VISUALLY RECEDE.

❋ THE BANQUETTES EACH HAVE ONE LARGE CENTRALLY PLACED TAPESTRY PILLOW.

❋ IDENTICAL REGENCY-STYLE CROSS-LEGGED TABLES ARE PLACED IN FRONT OF EACH BANQUETTE, COMPLETING THE MIRROR IMAGE OF THESE SEATING AREAS.

❋ ARTWORK CONSISTS OF A BALANCED CLUSTER OF LAND-SCAPE PAINTINGS IN GILT-AND-BLACK FRAMES AND ONE LARGE PAINTING ABOVE THE FIREPLACE.

❋ TWO ALABASTER LAMPS, ONE ON EACH SIDE OF THE FIRE-PLACE, PROVIDE ADDITIONAL LIGHTING.

❋ THE BLANKET ON THE RÉCAMIER IS ADDED AT THIS TIME, AS BY NOW THE ROOM'S OCCUPANT HAS DISCOVERED THIS GREAT FIRESIDE SPOT FOR READING.

❋ FLOWERS ON THE MANTEL AND A FEW DECORATIVE OBJECTS COMPLETE STAGE II.

"It was a rosy room, hung with one of the new English chintzes, which also covered the deep sofa" —EDITH WHARTON

STAGE III

T HE FINAL STAGE BRINGS A WEALTH OF WELL-BALANCED ACCESSORIES TO UNIFY THIS ROOM, WITH ITS POWERFUL SPATIAL CONFIGURATIONS.

* TWO TALL CANDLESTICKS WITH GLASS CHIMNEYS REST ON THE MANTEL.

* TWO ROSE BOWLS, SPILLING OVER WITH LARGE BLOOMS, SIT ON EITHER SIDE OF A FILLED OPENWORK SILVER BASKET ON THE MANTEL.

* A PAIR OF OVAL REGENCY-STYLE MIRRORS FILL THE VOID ON EACH SIDE OF THE FIREPLACE AND BALANCE THE LARGE PAINTING BETWEEN THEM, AS WELL AS ADDING CURVES WHERE RIGHT ANGLES DOMINATE. SILK PICTURE BOWS DISGUISE THE SUPPORT CHAINS THAT HANG FROM THE PICTURE MOLDING.

* PORCELAIN PLATES ON EASELS ARE PLACED ON THE CABINETS.

* A BOLSTER CUSHION BREAKS THE MONOTONY OF THE ELONGATED RÉCAMIER AND ADDS A FEELING OF INVITATION.

* A SMALL FOOTSTOOL PLACED UNDER THE DEMI-LUNE TABLE FILLS A VOID AND FURTHER BALANCES THE NEWLY ENHANCED ARRANGEMENT OF A LAMP, BOOKS, AND AN ORCHID ON THE TABLE ABOVE.

* THE FLORAL CHINTZ IN THE WINDOW TREATMENT PROVIDES LIGHTNESS AND MOVEMENT AROUND THE LARGE EXPANSE OF GLASS AND BALANCES THE LOVE SEAT IN THE CENTER. A CHINTZ WAS SELECTED FOR THE WINDOWS TO RELAX THE ROOM, AS PRINTS GENERALLY DO, WHEREAS A SILK STRIPE OR DAMASK WOULD FORMALIZE THE ROOM.

Variations

THE MANTEL IS CLEARED OF ANY OBJECTS AND VISUAL ATTENTION IS FOCUSED ON THIS GLASS-BORDERED MIRROR. IF THE MIRROR WERE PLACED MUCH HIGHER, THE MANTEL WOULD APPEAR VACANT, AS OPPOSED TO CLEAN. A PAIR OF WALL-MOUNTED BRACKETS, EACH CONTAINING A DOUBLE-HANDLED PORCELAIN URN, EXTEND SLIGHTLY BEYOND THE MANTEL AND KEEP THE ARRANGEMENT FROM BEING SQUARE. THE TOP OF THE URN IS INCHES ABOVE THE MIDDLE OF THE MIRROR, AGAIN PREVENTING SQUARENESS AND RIGIDITY.

A PAIR OF AMARYLLIS ARE POTTED IN PORCELAIN CACHEPOTS. A MIRROR FRAMED IN ORNATELY CARVED GILT WOOD HANGS IN THE CENTER. ON EACH SIDE OF THE MIRROR ARE HUNG A TRIO OF PORCELAIN PLATES, WHICH FRAME THE MIRROR AND CREATE A MORE HORIZONTAL ARRANGEMENT THAN THE ONE ABOVE. THE COMBINATION OF PLATES AND A MIRROR ALWAYS CREATES AN INTERESTING ARRANGEMENT AND CAN BE DONE ANY NUMBER OF WAYS. SKETCHING YOUR PROPOSED ARRANGEMENT ON PAPER WILL PREVENT YOU FROM MAKING TOO MANY HOLES IN THE WALL!

What to do with a fireplace mantel and the wall above is a dilemma most people would welcome. When there is a fireplace, it becomes a feature of great importance. The mantel is a perfect spot to display prized objects and favorite possessions.

A PEDESTAL URN IS POSITIONED ON EACH SIDE OF THE MANTEL. THE FLOWERS IN THESE URNS ARE MADE OF PAINTED TOLE. A LARGE LANDSCAPE PAINTING IS HUNG ABOUT SIX INCHES ABOVE THE MANTEL. THE SCALE, DEPTH OF COLOR, AND IMPORTANCE OF THIS PAINTING REQUIRE THAT IT NOT REST ON THE MANTEL. ALSO, BECAUSE THIS PAINTING IS THE LARGEST IN THE ROOM AND IS VIEWED IMMEDIATELY UPON ENTERING, IT EASILY STANDS ON ITS OWN, DRAWING EACH VISITOR INTO ITS CLOUDY VISTA.

A RECTANGULAR PLANTER, FILLED WITH FLOWERS, IS FLANKED BY A PAIR OF GILT METAL CANDLESTICK LAMPS DECORATED WITH PORCELAIN FLOWERS. A ROUND MIRROR CARVED WITH FRUITS AND FLOWERS ADDS CURVES ABOVE THE HORIZONTAL LINE OF THE MANTEL. THE FLORAL MOTIFS AND GOLD DETAILS OF THESE OBJECTS REINFORCE EACH OTHER. AMPLE SPACE BETWEEN THE MIRROR AND THE MANTEL ENSURES BOTH THE MIRROR'S INDEPENDENT SUPPORT AND SPACE BELOW IT FOR A CENTERPIECE THAT DOES NOT OBSCURE ITS DETAILS.

Color Palette:

Delphinium

Jade

Cherry

Fabrics:

Floral—curtains, bed curtains, bed skirt, headboard

Large plaid—banquette pillows, tufted bench

Green velvet—banquette, armchairs

Red check—dressing table skirt, balloon shades

Blue check—Regency-style chairs, blanket cover

Green check—dressing table chair

Paint:

Decorator's white—trim and ceiling

A New Angle in the Master Bedroom

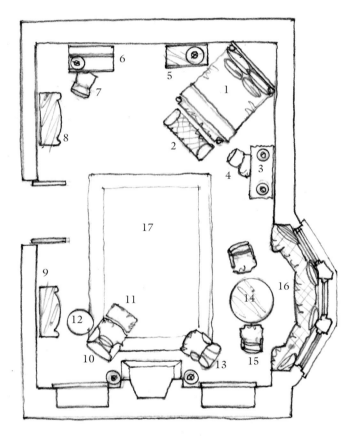

1. FOUR-POSTER BED 2. UPHOLSTERED BENCH
3. DRESSING TABLE 4. CHAIR 5. NIGHTSTAND
6. SECRETARY 7. DESK CHAIR 8. CHEST OF DRAWERS
9. ÉTAGÈRE 10. UPHOLSTERED READING CHAIR
11. OTTOMAN 12. BOOK BASKET 13. FIRESIDE SLIPPER CHAIR
14. ROUND BREAKFAST TABLE 15. ARMCHAIRS
16. BUILT-IN WINDOW SEAT 17. NEEDLEPOINT RUG

STAGE I

THE FURNITURE SELECTION AND PLACEMENT HERE ALLOW THIS BEDROOM TO BE USED FOR MULTIPLE FUNCTIONS— DINING, READING, VISITING, A PLACE FOR AN IMPROMPTU HOME OFFICE, DRESSING AND APPLYING MAKEUP, AND, OF COURSE, SLEEP- ING. ON THE BED SIDE OF THE ROOM IS A TALL SECRETARY (VISIBLE ONLY IN THE FLOOR PLAN), WHICH ADDS THE BALANCE NEEDED TO OFFSET THE HEIGHT OF THE BED. FURNITURE IS RELEGATED TO THE PERIMETER OF THE ROOM, LEAVING THE CENTRAL FLOOR SPACE FREE FOR EASY PASSAGE.

⚜ THE PLACEMENT OF THE LARGE MAHOGANY FOUR-POSTER BED AT AN ANGLE IN THE CORNER OF THIS BEDROOM NOT ONLY CREATES A NEW PER- SPECTIVE BUT ALSO MAKES THE BED THE ROOM'S UNMISTAKABLE FOCAL POINT. THE MASS AND VERTICALITY OF THE BED ALSO EMPHASIZE AND UTI- LIZE THE GENEROUS CEILING HEIGHT.

⚜ A WINDOW SEAT WITH A ROUND TABLE AND A PAIR OF REGENCY-STYLE SIDE CHAIRS CREATE A NOOK FOR AN EARLY-MORNING BREAKFAST OR A SUN-FILLED SPOT IN WHICH TO SIT AND TACKLE CORRESPONDENCE.

⚜ A SKIRTED DRESSING TABLE IS PLACED NEXT TO THE WINDOW TO TAKE ADVANTAGE OF NATURAL LIGHT AND TO DOUBLE AS A BEDSIDE TABLE.

⚜ A PAINTED WHITE SIDE CHAIR IS PLACED IN FRONT OF THE DRESSING TABLE.

⚜ VELVET ARMCHAIRS FOR READING ARE POSITIONED ACROSS FROM THE BED.

⚜ A PAINTED BEDSIDE TABLE WITH A DRAWER STANDS READY.

⚜ THE CARPET IS WOVEN WITH A GEOMETRIC PATTERN.

STAGE II

THE CHEERFUL COLOR SCHEME OF JADE, DELPHINIUM, WHITE, AND CHERRY HARMONIOUSLY INJECTS THIS SPACE WITH BOLD DASHES OF COLOR AGAINST A PREDOMINANTLY WHITE GROUND. THE VARIOUS PATTERNS USED ON THE FABRICS—FLORAL, CHECK, PLAID—COMPLEMENT ONE ANOTHER BY UTILIZING THE SAME COLOR SCHEME.

❧ THE WINDOW SEAT IS NOW UPHOLSTERED IN PLUSH GREEN VELVET WITH COORDINATING PLAID PILLOWS.

❧ ON THE TOP OF THE DRESSING TABLE, THE ESSENTIALS—LAMPS AND A MIRROR—ARE APPROPRIATELY PLACED. AN ARRANGEMENT OF THREE BOTANICAL WATERCOLORS COMPLETES THIS CORNER.

❧ A LIDDED BASKET CONTAINING NEEDLEWORK AND BOOKS ALSO SERVES AS AN IMPROMPTU END TABLE.

❧ A VIVID FLORAL DRESSES THE UPHOLSTERED HEADBOARD, BED CURTAINS, AND BED SKIRT. A SOLID PALE GREEN IS USED FOR THE LINING OF THE BED CURTAINS. A PLAIN WHITE PIQUÉ BEDCOVER EMBROIDERED WITH A SCALLOPING DETAIL IN PINK COVERS THE BED.

❧ A WOODEN COLUMN LAMP PAINTED GREEN AND TOPPED WITH A RUFFLED SILK SHADE ILLUMINATES THE BEDSIDE TABLE.

"I believe that everything in one's house should be comfortable, but one's bedroom must be more than comfortable: it must be intimate."

—ELSIE DE WOLFE

STAGE III

A T THE LAST STAGE, CURTAINS ARE ADDED TO THE WINDOWS AND AN AREA RUG IS PLACED ON THE OTHER SIDE OF THE ROOM. IT IS THE STYLE OF THE VARIOUS PERSONAL OBJECTS THAT GIVES THIS MOST PERSONAL OF ROOMS, THE BEDROOM, ITS DISTINCTIVE FLAIR.

❧ THE WINDOW IS OUTLINED IN FLORAL CURTAINS ON A MAHOGANY POLE. A SWAG IN THE SAME FABRIC STRETCHES ACROSS EACH PANEL AND IS FINISHED WITH WHITE FRINGE TO EMPHASIZE AND ADD WEIGHT TO THE DRAPE. THE CURTAINS ARE HELD TO THE SIDE BY GREEN ROPE TIEBACKS. THE SAME WHITE FRINGE ON THE DRAPE IS USED AT THE HEM AND DRAWS ATTENTION TO THE SOFT PUDDLING EFFECT OF THE CURTAINS ON THE FLOOR. AS THESE CURTAINS WERE NOT MADE TO BE DRAWN, THEY GIVE MAXIMUM EFFECT WITH A MINIMUM OF FABRIC. THIS TECHNIQUE OF STATIONARY PANELS IS OFTEN EMPLOYED WHEN ANOTHER WINDOW TREATMENT IS USED. IN THIS CASE, BALLOON SHADES, IN THE SAME SMALL CHERRY CHECK AS THE DRESSING TABLE SKIRT, ARE HUNG INSIDE THE WINDOWS.

❧ A DARK NEEDLEPOINT CARPET PLACED AT AN ANGLE ADDS DEPTH OF COLOR AND WEIGHT TO AN OTHERWISE LIGHT FLOOR. THE RUG ALSO DEFINES THE AREA WHERE THE CLUB CHAIR IS CENTRAL AND BREAKS THE LARGE EXPANSE OF THIS PATTERNED CARPET.

❧ A SCROLL ARM DEEP-BUTTONED BENCH COVERED IN PLAID PROVIDES A PLACE TO SIT WHILE PUTTING ON SHOES, TO STACK A FEW MAGAZINES, AND TO STORE EXTRA PILLOWS WHILE SLEEPING.

❧ A COUPLE OF ADDITIONAL BOTANICAL PRINTS HAVE EXPANDED THE EXISTING COLLECTION.

❧ FAMILY PHOTOS, AS WELL AS OTHER PERSONAL OBJECTS, HAVE BEEN ADDED TO THE BEDSIDE TABLE.

❧ A CLUSTER OF PILLOWS AND A BLUE CHECK BLANKET COVER ON THE BED AWAIT THIS RESIDENT.

Variations

WHEN YOU REMOVE THE BENCH FROM THE FOOT OF THE BED AND REPLACE THE FLORAL PRINT WITH THIS VIBRANT PLAID, A TOTALLY DIFFERENT, MORE CASUAL LOOK IS CREATED.

THE SKIRTED DRESSING TABLE HAS BEEN RE-PLACED BY A CLEAN-LINED DESK, CREATING A PLACE TO WORK. A SINGLE COLUMN-SHAPED TABLE LAMP REPLACES THE PAIR OF CANDLESTICK LAMPS, AND THE TWO OVAL FLORAL PRINTS HUNG DIRECTLY ABOVE ADD A QUIET NOTE OF VERTICAL-ITY TO THE HORIZONTAL PLANE OF THE DESK.

Seasonal or stylistic variations can easily be produced when patterns and colors are changed. Do not be afraid to mix different patterns, as long as the color palette remains the unifying factor.

FULL GATHERED CURTAINS IN PALE JADE ARE JOINED IN THE CENTER WITH A SUBTLE ROSETTE. FLORAL BALLOON SHADES, WHICH BALANCE THE BED AND PUT WEIGHT BENEATH THE LIGHT CURTAINS, CAN AGAIN BE LOWERED FOR PRIVACY. GREEN VELVET ON THE WINDOW SEAT BALANCES THE GREEN CLUB CHAIR IN FRONT OF THE FIREPLACE AND ADDS WEIGHT BENEATH THIS ELABORATE WINDOW TREATMENT. PILLOWS MADE FROM THE CHINTZ COMBINED WITH A FEW ODD NEEDLEPOINT CUSHIONS LIGHTEN THE VELVET CUSHION AND UNIFY THE CORNER. THE DARK PAINTED CHAIRS HAVE BEEN REPLACED WITH FRENCH SIDE CHAIRS COVERED IN THE SAME FLORAL CHINTZ.

A GREEN VELVET CHAISE REPLACES THE BUILT-IN WINDOW SEAT IN FRONT OF THE WINDOW. A PLAID VALANCE HANGS ABOVE SIMPLE TAILORED CURTAINS IN THE SAME FABRIC. UNLINED BALLOON SHADES IN A PALE JADE GREEN PROVIDE A SOFT BACKGROUND FOR THE PLAID, ALLOW MAXIMUM LIGHT, AND WHEN DROPPED GIVE NEEDED PRIVACY. AN OPENWORK WIRE BASKET WITH A SPRINGTIME FLORAL ARRANGEMENT IS PLACED ON THE SILL. ONE VERY SOFT TAPESTRY PILLOW PROVIDES EXTRA COMFORT AND INTEREST TO THIS LONG STRETCH OF GREEN VELVET. A LAP BLANKET SITS POISED FOR THAT AFTERNOON NAP.

Color Palette:

Beige

Leaf

Ivory

Natural

Fabrics:

Plaid—armchair, curtains, headboard, bed curtains, bed skirt

Cotton moiré—bed curtain lining

Woven natural—bed coverlet

Beige scroll—bench

Woven taupe—desk chairs

Paint:

Beige—walls

White—trim and ceiling

A Soothing Master Bedroom Suite

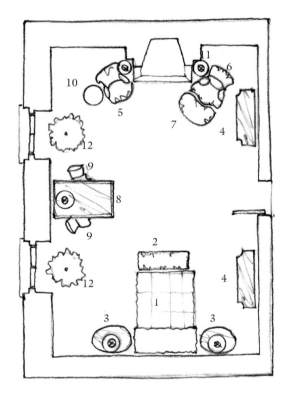

1. QUEEN-SIZE BED WITH CORONA
2. UPHOLSTERED BENCH 3. PAIR OF PAINTED
AND TIERED BEDSIDE TABLES
4. PAIR OF TALL BOOKCASES
5. LADY'S UPHOLSTERED CLUB CHAIR
6. GENTLEMAN'S UPHOLSTERED CLUB CHAIR
7. OTTOMAN 8. WRITING DESK 9. DESK CHAIR
10. SMALL SIDE TABLE 11. SWING-ARM LAMPS
12. PAIR OF POTTED BAY TREES

STAGE I

IN THIS BEDROOM, THE BED IS PLACED IN A MORE TRADITIONAL MANNER, ON THE LARGEST EXPANSE OF WALL, AND IS DIRECTLY OPPOSITE A FIREPLACE. THE FEW PIECES OF FURNITURE HAVE BEEN CAREFULLY CHOSEN FOR A CLEAN, PARED-DOWN ENVIRONMENT AND ARE LOCATED AROUND THE PERIMETER. A WRITING TABLE PROVIDES WORK SPACE FOR BOTH RESIDENTS, AND A PAIR OF BOOKCASES ALLOWS ONE FOR EACH.

A LARGE ROOM LIKE THIS DOES NOT NECESSARILY HAVE TO BE FILLED WITH FURNITURE. ONCE BASIC NEEDS ARE MET, IT IS OKAY TO STOP THERE, EVEN THOUGH THE ROOM MIGHT LOOK A LITTLE BARE.

❧ THE BED VALANCE NOT ONLY ADDS IMPORTANCE IN THIS MASTER BEDROOM, IT ALSO SERVES TO SOFTEN THE WALL BEHIND AND PROVIDE ANOTHER WAY TO USE FABRIC TO STRENGTHEN THE SCHEME OF THE ROOM.

❧ DEEP-SET WINDOWS ARE SHUTTERED TO PROVIDE PRIVACY AND AT THE SAME TIME ADMIT LIGHT.

❧ A NATURAL FLAT-WOVEN SISAL FLOOR COVERING ADDS TEXTURE AND HELPS ESTABLISH A CASUAL AND ALMOST TROPICAL FEELING IN THIS SPACE.

❧ A PAINTED FRENCH-STYLE DESK IS PAIRED WITH TWO UPHOLSTERED FRENCH ARMCHAIRS OPPOSITE THE BED.

❧ TWO TIERED BEDSIDE TABLES PROVIDE PLENTY OF SPACE FOR LAMPS, PHOTOS, BOOKS, AND A FRESH BOUQUET OF FLOWERS.

STAGE II

W ITH THE BED, SIDE TABLES, AND DESK NOW IN PLACE WE ARE READY TO ADD MORE LIFE TO THE ROOM. THE OVERALL EFFECT OF LIMITING THE COLOR SCHEME TO A COUPLE OF COLORS WITH LOW CONTRAST, AND OF REPEATING FABRICS, NOT ONLY IS EASY ON THE EYE BUT ALSO CREATES THE SOOTHING AMBIENCE GENERALLY SOUGHT IN A MASTER BEDROOM.

❧ TO VISUALLY EXPAND THE SIZE OF THIS ROOM AND TO PROVIDE A PEACEFUL, SOOTHING BACKGROUND, THE WALLS ARE PAINTED IN A LIGHT BEIGE. SIMPLE MOLDINGS AT THE CEILING LINE ARE PAINTED WHITE TO BLEND WITH THE CEILING.

❧ THE SHUTTERS ARE PAINTED WHITE TO GENTLY FRAME THE ROOM AND TO GIVE ONLY SUBTLE CONTRAST TO THE COLOR OF THE WALLS.

❧ A LARGE PLAID IN LEAF GREEN, WHITE, AND BEIGE IS USED FOR THE BED CURTAINS, SKIRT, AND UPHOLSTERED HEADBOARD. A NATURAL WOVEN COVERLET SOFTLY COORDINATES WITH THE PLAID FABRIC AND INTRODUCES ADDITIONAL TEXTURE.

❧ A LARGE RECTANGULAR WOODEN MIRROR HANGS ABOVE THE DESK, ADDING A FOCAL POINT TO THE WALL, DRAMATIC COLOR CONTRAST, AND THE TEXTURE OF NATURAL WOOD.

❧ NUMEROUS GROUPINGS OF ENGRAVINGS AND SEPIA PRINTS IN PALE OR PASTEL MATS AND VARIOUS STYLES OF GILT FRAMES GIVE ADDITIONAL IMPORTANCE TO THE BED WALL AND FURTHER ACCENTUATE THE HEIGHT OF THIS WELCOMING BED.

❧ A TOLE URN LAMP WITH A SIMPLE PARCHMENT SHADE IS PLACED ON EITHER SIDE OF THE BED. THE DESK HOLDS A BRASS BOULLIOTTE LAMP WITH A TRADITIONAL TOLE SHADE.

"Color should never be allowed to get the best of a house

STAGE III

SIMPLE, NATURAL COLORS, THE FRESHNESS OF GREEN, AND THE COMBINATION OF TEXTURE AND CLEAN-LINED FURNITURE PROVIDE THE PERFECT ELEMENTS FOR A SUNNY, SOOTHING, AND WELCOMING BEDROOM.

◈ CURTAINS AND VALANCES THAT MIMIC THE STYLE OF THE BED AND CORONA ARE ADDED, TO WARM AND SOFTEN THE DEEP RECESS OF THE SHUTTERED WINDOWS. REPEATING THE STYLES ALLOWS THE ROOM TO MAINTAIN ITS SIMPLICITY.

◈ A PORCELAIN PLATE ON AN EASEL, PHOTOS, BOOKS, AND FLOWERS WARM THE BEDSIDE TABLES AND BRING MORE PERSONALITY INTO THE ROOM. A PAINTING OF A SINGLE FLOWER IS CASUALLY DISPLAYED, RESTING ATOP A BEDSIDE TABLE.

◈ PICTURES ADDED TO THE WALL LEFT OF THE WINDOW EXTEND THE EXISTING ARRANGEMENT.

◈ AN ADDITIONAL PICTURE IS PLACED ABOVE THE MIRROR. THIS NOT ONLY SYNCHRONIZES THIS WALL WITH THE OTHERS, IT DRAWS THE EYE HIGHER AND SETS THE STAGE FOR SMALLER ADDITIONAL PICTURES TO BE ADDED LATER TO EACH SIDE OF THE MIRROR.

◈ A HAND-PAINTED CERAMIC POT FILLED WITH A BAY TREE IS PLACED IN FRONT OF THE LIGHT SOURCE AND BRINGS THE OUTDOORS INSIDE.

◈ THE FRENCH-STYLE BENCH NOW AT THE FOOT OF THE BED IS THE IDEAL PLACE TO SET DOWN A BREAKFAST TRAY OR TO SERVE AS VALET FOR CLOTHING WHILE YOU DRESS.

or room."—ELSIE DE WOLFE

Variations

The beige scroll fabric is used on this upholstered headboard and bed skirt. Large green silk tasseled tiebacks add another decorative element. Pillows covered in the beige scroll fabric are finished in a contrasting silk fringe of leaf green and ivory. The large plaid fabric is used for the coverlet as well as for the simple bowed corona. Using the same casual-style plaid on this corona, but in a different scale and configuration, would dress down this formal bed.

The valance and curtains have been removed and the walls have been painted leaf green to create crisp contrast. The button-tufted headboard is softly shaped and covered in the beige scroll fabric. This same fabric is used in the gathered bed skirt. A natural woven coverlet finishes this warm, monochromatic scheme. A dash of additional color is provided by the round floral still life hung by a beige silk ribbon, which nicely masks the picture wire.

When you change the headboard style, the fabrics, the wall color, and the shape of the corona, you can create many different effects. These variations can either give importance to the bed or give it equal standing with the rest of the furniture.

Here, the beige scroll fabric is used again for the valance and bed curtains. Bows accent the top of the valance for a more feminine treatment. The plaid is used on the box-pleated tailored bed skirt, the tiebacks, and the padded headboard in a straight-edged shape with scalloped corners. Limited use of the plaid adds some contrast to this otherwise monochromatic ensemble.

The walls have been covered in plaid, which creates a coziness and richness in the room. The beige scroll fabric is used on the arched and padded headboard and valance, as well as on the bed curtains and skirt. As the plaid fabric on the walls creates a multitude of lines, the arch of the corona softens and de-emphasizes them. Green silk fringe outlines the soft folds and lines of the curtains. Plaid pillow shams add punch.

Color Palette:

Beige

Ivory

Black

Fabrics:

Woven toile—bench

Black-and-white plaid—chair in front of chest

Black-and-white check—window treatments

Tan-and-black woven linen—armchairs flanking fireplace

Paint:

Beige—walls

Taupe—trim

China white—ceiling

A Gentleman's Library/Retreat

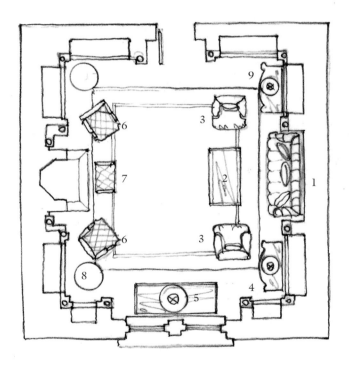

1. DEEP-BUTTONED LEATHER SOFA 2. COFFEE TABLE
3. PAIR OF UPHOLSTERED CLUB CHAIRS
4. SMALL CHEST 5. ROSEWOOD CHEST
6. PAIR OF MAHOGANY AND CANE ENGLISH ARMCHAIRS
7. X-SHAPED BENCH 8. ANTIQUE GLOBE 9. SOFA TABLE

STAGE I

A SQUARE ROOM ALWAYS PRESENTS A CHAL-LENGE BUT IS ESPECIALLY PROBLEMATIC WHEN THE CORNERS ARE LINED WITH MASSIVE BOOK-CASES AND A LARGE FIREPLACE DOMINATES ONE WALL. THE FURNITURE MUST BE PLACED TO PROVIDE EASY ACCESS TO THE BOOKCASES AND COMFORTABLE SEAT-ING AT THE FIREPLACE. THE CENTRAL FLOOR AREA IS KEPT FREE TO FACILITATE MOVEMENT AND AN UNOB-STRUCTED ENTRY. THE FIREPLACE SERVES AS THE FOCAL POINT OF THE ROOM.

❧ HARDWOOD FLOORS ARE PARTIALLY COVERED WITH A RUG, WHICH ADDS WARMTH BUT AT THE SAME TIME ALLOWS THE RICHNESS OF THE WOODEN FLOOR TO PLAY A KEY ROLE IN THIS VERY MASCULINE ROOM.

❧ READING CHAIRS FLANK THE FIREPLACE AND A BENCH ADDS ANOTHER PLACE TO SIT OR TO PROP YOUR FEET.

❧ A ROSEWOOD CHEST SITS IN FRONT OF THE WINDOW AND IS SEEN IMMEDIATELY UPON ENTERING.

❧ THE SEATING AREA ACROSS FROM THE FIREPLACE COM-PRISES A TUFTED SOFA AND A PAIR OF OVERSTUFFED CLUB CHAIRS FACING EACH OTHER, WITH A MARBLE-TOPPED COFFEE TABLE IN THE MIDDLE.

STAGE II

I N THIS SUBDUED COLOR SCHEME, THE WALLS
ARE PAINTED A NEUTRAL GRAY-BEIGE, WHILE
THE BOOKCASES AND MOLDING ARE PAINTED A
SLIGHTLY DARKER SHADE.

❧ THE PILASTERS ARE FINISHED WITH BRASS AT THE BASE AND
AT THE CAPITALS, WHICH MAKES THE BOOKCASES LOOK MORE
LIKE IMPORTANT PIECES OF FURNITURE THAN BUILT-INS.

❧ THE CHEST NOW HOLDS A LARGE ETRUSCAN-STYLE JAR
MADE INTO A LAMP.

❧ A LIDDED WOODEN BOX HAS BEEN PLACED ON THE COFFEE
TABLE TO HOLD PLAYING CARDS AND POKER CHIPS. ANOTHER
BOX, OF TORTOISESHELL, IS ON THE MANTEL.

"A man travels the world over in search of what he needs and

returns home to find it.”
—GEORGE MOORE

STAGE III

A T THIS STAGE, THE GENTLEMAN MAY INFUSE THE ROOM WITH FAMILY PHOTOS, ANTIQUES, BOOKS, AND ITEMS THAT INDICATE HIS PERSONAL INTERESTS IN ART, ANTIQUES, HISTORY, OR HIS FAMILY.

◈ AN ANTIQUE GLOBE ON A MAHOGANY STAND IS PLACED IN THE CORNER.

◈ THE BLACK MARBLE FIREPLACE MANTEL IS TOPPED BY A PAIR OF MARBLE URNS, AND THE TORTOISESHELL BOX HAS BEEN OPENED AND PLANTED WITH ORCHIDS.

◈ AN OVERSIZE BULL'S-EYE MIRROR HANGS ABOVE THE FIRE-PLACE AND PROVIDES A NICE CONTRAST TO ALL THE VERTI-CAL LINES

◈ HANDSOME LEATHER-BOUND BOOKS FILL THE SHELVES.

◈ THE BOOKSHELVES HAVE BEEN TRIMMED WITH LEATHER SHELF EDGING.

◈ PORCELAIN PLATES HAVE BEEN ADDED TO THE TOP SHELF OF THE BOOKCASE.

◈ A PAIR OF CANDLESTICKS AND A PAIR OF DECORATIVE PLATES ON THE COFFEE TABLE CREATE A BALANCED ARRANGE-MENT IN THIS ORDERED AND REFINED ROOM.

◈ THE BOLD BLACK-AND-WHITE CHECK USED AT THE WIN-DOW REITERATES THE ROOM'S PREDOMINANTLY MASCULINE SCHEME.

Variations

THE ROSEWOOD CHEST IS REPLACED WITH A THREE-TIERED SERVER, ALSO CALLED A WHATNOT. THE BOTTOM TWO TIERS ARE FILLED WITH BOOKS, AND THE TOP SHELF CONTAINS AN ALABASTER LAMP WITH A SOFTLY GATHERED SILK SHADE. BULLION FRINGE IN SHADES OF TAUPE AND CREAM OUTLINES AND ADDS WEIGHT TO THE PLAID OUTSIDE CURTAIN. A NATURAL-COLOR UNDERCURTAIN IS SECURED WITH ROPE AND TASSEL TIEBACKS. THIS WINDOW TREATMENT IS LIGHT, YET AS HIGHLY DETAILED AS THE REST OF THE ROOM.

HERE, THE CHEST IS REPLACED WITH A BANQUETTE COVERED IN A WOVEN BLACK-AND-WHITE TOILE. THIS PLACEMENT ALLOWS ONE TO TAKE ADVANTAGE OF NATURAL LIGHT FOR READING. DARK NEEDLEPOINT CUSHIONS PROVIDE CONTRAST AGAINST THE LIGHT GROUND OF THIS FABRIC. CREAM-COLORED CURTAINS WITH GENTLE PLEATS PROVIDE A LIGHT FRAME FOR DARK WOODEN BLINDS.

If a fireplace is present, it is very often the focal point of a room. The mantel, therefore, should be reserved as a place for important or interesting art and objects. At the same time, because the window is the first thing viewed upon entering this room, alternative treatments and uses of this space are suggested. Variations can also be achieved by simply rearranging your furniture.

INSTEAD OF THE ROUND MIRROR A LARGE OIL PAINTING OF A HORSE IN A CARVED FRAME HANGS ABOVE THE MANTELPIECE. A BRASS PLANTER RESTS BETWEEN A SET OF BRASS CANDLESTICKS WITH GLASS CHIMNEYS. THE BRASS AND GILT SOFTEN AND BRIGHTEN THIS SCHEME OF BLACKS AND BROWNS.

A PAIR OF BASALT DOLPHIN CANDLESTICKS FLANK AN EBONY-AND-ORMOLU MANTEL CLOCK. THE BLACK REINFORCES THE EXISTING SCHEME AND ALMOST ACTS AS AN EXTENSION OF THE MANTEL. A LARGE ANTIQUE MAP IS ENCASED IN A GILT FRAME WITH CLEAN LINES. THE DETAIL IN ALL THESE OBJECTS MIGHT BE OVERLOOKED IF THE FRAME WERE MORE ORNATE.

Color Palette:

Cinnabar

Cream

Fabrics:

Cinnabar-and-cream toile—sofa, table skirt, Roman shades

Cinnabar-and-cream windowpane check—lounge chairs

Woven solid cinnabar—wicker dining chairs

Paint:

Celadon—walls and ceiling

Cream—trim

A Sun-Filled
Family Porch

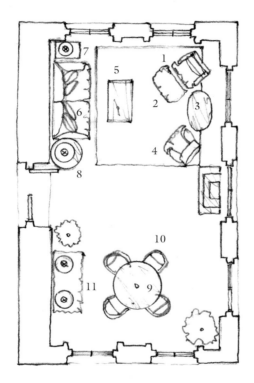

1. WICKER CLUB CHAIR 2. OTTOMAN
3. OVAL WICKER TABLE 4. UPHOLSTERED
CLUB CHAIR 5. WICKER COFFEE TABLE
6. LOVE SEAT 7. WICKER SIDE TABLE
8. PAINTED ROUND PEDESTAL TABLE
9. PAINTED ROUND DINING TABLE
10. WICKER DINING CHAIRS
11. SKIRTED TABLE

STAGE I

T HE PLACEMENT OF FURNITURE IN THIS MULTIPURPOSE FAMILY ROOM DEFINES TWO DISTINCT AREAS. THE MAIN SEATING AREA IS ESTABLISHED BY A LOVE SEAT, A WICKER CHAIR WITH CUSHIONS, A CLUB CHAIR, AND A WICKER COFFEE TABLE. A SECONDARY DINING AREA IS CREATED AROUND A CIRCULAR TABLE PLACED BENEATH AN EIGHT-ARM CHANDELIER. A DRAPED SIDE TABLE PLACED AGAINST THE WALL WILL SERVE A NUMBER OF NEEDS. THIS ARRANGEMENT ALLOWS FOR SIMULTANEOUS FAMILY ACTIVITIES TO TAKE PLACE.

❧ SEVEN SETS OF FRENCH DOORS LINE THE PERIMETER OF THE ROOM AND PROVIDE AN ABUNDANCE OF LIGHT, AIR, AND EASY ACCESS TO THE YARD AND GARDENS.

❧ EXPOSED BEAMS ON THE CEILING ADD A CASUAL ELEMENT TO THIS INDOOR/OUTDOOR ROOM.

❧ THE FLOOR IS MADE OF LARGE LIMESTONE SQUARES.

❧ THE SIDE TABLES PLACED BETWEEN THE WICKER CHAIRS AND NEXT TO THE LOVE SEAT ARE PAINTED IN A RUSTIC DARK FINISH AND BEAR MARBLE TOPS FOR DURABILITY.

STAGE II

I N THIS STAGE, BURSTS OF COLOR APPEAR ON PILLOWS, SEAT CUSHIONS, AND LAMPSHADES. THESE ACCENTS ADD WARMTH IN CONTRAST TO THE LIMESTONE FLOOR AND THE COOL CELADON WALLS AND CEILING.

⁂ THE WALLS AND CEILING ARE PAINTED THE PALEST SHADE OF CELADON, WHICH REFLECTS NATURAL LIGHT, TO CREATE A SUNNY SPOT.

⁂ THE CINNABAR-AND-CREAM TOILE COVERING THE LOVE SEAT ALSO COVERS THE RECTANGULAR TABLE. THIS SKIRTING ALLOWS FOR ADDITIONAL STORAGE UNDERNEATH AND AT THE SAME TIME SOFTENS THE LINES AND LEGGINESS OF THIS CORNER OF THE ROOM. A CASUAL BAR SETUP IS ON THE TABLE, WITH A PAIR OF BRASS CANDLESTICK LAMPS TOPPED WITH PARCHMENT SHADES.

⁂ ACCESSORIES ARE REFLECTIVE OF THE GARDENS AND OUTDOORS AND CONSIST OF PLANTS, URNS, AND A SUNBURST MIRROR.

⁂ A TOLE COLUMN LAMP NEXT TO THE SOFA HAS A HEXAGONAL CARD SHADE WITH HAND-PAINTED FLOWERS.

⁂ A PAIR OF PILLOWS IN A SOLID WOVEN CINNABAR FABRIC HAVE BEEN ADDED TO THE SOFA FOR COMFORT AND FOR AN EXTRA PUNCH OF COLOR.

STAGE III

T OPIARIES AND FLOWERING PLANTS COMPLEMENT THE ROOM'S INDOOR/OUTDOOR FEELING. THESE INVITING FINAL TOUCHES ENSURE THAT THIS WILL BE A PERENNIAL FAVORITE AS THE MOST COMFORTABLE AND FUNCTIONAL ROOM IN THE HOUSE.

❀ A LARGE ANTIQUE BAROMETER IS ADDED ABOVE THE SKIRTED TABLE, BALANCING THE MIRROR ON THE OTHER SIDE OF THE WALL.

❀ TWO BLACK-AND-WHITE FIGURAL ENGRAVINGS HANG JUST BELOW THE MIRROR, FILLING THE GAPS IN EACH CORNER BUT LEAVING ROOM FOR FUTURE ADDITIONS.

❀ A PAIR OF LARGE GREEN PILLOWS ARE ADDED TO THE SOFA. THE GREEN PILLOWS BREAK UP THE MONOTONY OF THE REDS AND MAKE THE ARRANGEMENT MORE LIVELY.

❀ THE WINDOW TREATMENTS ARE SIMPLE ROMAN SHADES IN THE SAME CINNABAR-AND-CREAM TOILE AS ON THE SOFA AND IN THE TABLE SKIRT. THE SHADES ALLOW UNINTERRUPTED VIEWS TO THE GARDEN AND ADD SOME SOFTNESS TO THIS LARGE EXPANSE OF WOOD AND GLASS. AT NIGHT, THEY ARE EASILY LOWERED TO PROVIDE PRIVACY.

❀ URNS NOW FILLED WITH PLANTS, VASES FILLED WITH FLOWERS FROM THE GARDEN, AND A BOWL FILLED WITH FRUIT MAKE THE ROOM READY FOR RELAXATION AND A SMALL SNACK.

❀ THE USE OF TWO RUGS FURTHER DEFINES THE TWO AREAS OF THE ROOM AND ALLOWS GREATER FLEXIBILITY IN THE EVENT ONE NEEDS TO BE CHANGED.

❀ SISAL WAS USED ON THE FLOOR FOR EASY MAINTENANCE, FOR TEXTURE, AND TO FURTHER PROMOTE THE FEELING OF OUTDOORS. SEA GRASS CAN EASILY BE SUBSTITUTED AND WILL PROVIDE THE SAME RESULTS.

"A house should be about living." —ALI MACGRAW

Variations

THE SOFA IS COVERED HERE IN A WOVEN WINDOWPANE-PLAID FABRIC. KNIFE-EDGE PILLOWS OF TOILE AND SOLID CINNABAR BRING THREE OF THE ROOM'S FABRICS TO THIS CORNER, AND A LARGE OIL LANDSCAPE HANGS ABOVE.

THE SOFA IS COVERED IN A WOVEN SOLID CINNABAR FABRIC, WITH CONTRASTING CREAM-COLORED PIPING FOR DETAIL. TWO DARK TAPESTRY PILLOWS ACT AS ANCHORS TO THE DARKER OBJECTS ABOVE. A LARGE BLACK-AND-WHITE ENGRAVING IS CENTERED ABOVE THE SOFA: TWO BRACKETS ARE HUNG ALONGSIDE, AND ON TOP OF EACH BRACKET ARE GLOBES ON PEDESTALS. A TOLE CLOCK COMPLETES THE ARRANGEMENT BY BRINGING THE EYE FARTHER UP THE WALL AND PREVENTING THE ARRANGEMENT FROM BEING FLAT-TOPPED AND SQUARE. THE BLACK IN THE CLOCK, FRAME, AND PILLOWS MAKES THE RED SOFA STAND OUT EVEN MORE.

Light versus dark, symmetry versus asymmetry—these are issues we confront in every room we decorate. Here are a few approaches that also suit this room very well.

Here the rectangular bar table is draped in a fabric with corner pleats and is topped by a pair of tole column lamps with shades created from old maps. A footed tole urn filled with flowers sits below a large watercolor of a house in a landscape.

The antique barometer hangs above the painted console table, now without its drape. Piles of books, a boulliotte lamp with a red tole shade, a mantel clock, and a plant in a natural wicker basket create an interesting mix on this tabletop. A large lidded rush basket sits underneath to fill the empty space and to provide possible storage needed for books, magazines, or toys.

Color Palette

Pomegranate

Willow

Ivory

Buttercup

Sage

Fabrics:

Plaid—Roman shades

Ikat—armchairs, chair next to sofa on the right, banquette cushion

Green velvet—sofa, ottoman, button-tufted armchairs

Paint:

Sage green—walls

Bone white and bone white
flat—trim and ceiling

An Architecturally Inspired Living Room

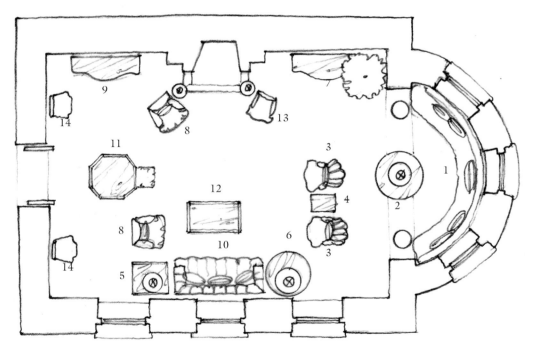

1. WINDOW SEAT 2. ROUND PEDESTAL TABLE 3. PAIR OF DEEP-BUTTONED UPHOLSTERED
ARMCHAIRS 4. TIERED SIDE TABLE 5. SQUARE SOFA TABLE 6. ROUND TRIPOD TABLE
7. MAHOGANY CHEST 8. CLUB CHAIR 9. MAHOGANY ARMOIRE 10. SOFA
11. OCTAGONAL PEDESTAL CENTER TABLE 12. BENCH/COFFEE TABLE 13. SCOTTISH ARMCHAIR
14. PAIR OF TALL NEEDLEPOINT SIDE CHAIRS

STAGE I

ARCHITECTURAL ELEMENTS DOMINATE THIS LIVING ROOM, WITH ITS EXTRAORDINARY CEILING HEIGHT. THE TALL, DEEP-SET WINDOWS ADMIT MAXIMUM LIGHT. THE WINDOW ALCOVE IS FITTED WITH A WINDOW SEAT, AND LARGE IONIC COLUMNS FLANK THE OPENING TO CREATE A BREAK IN THE VAST EXPANSE OF THE ROOM AND TO DRAW ATTENTION TO THE CEILING. AN EXCEPTIONALLY DEEP CROWN MOLDING SURROUNDS THE ROOM AT THE CEILING LINE.

- A BUTTON-TUFTED CHESTERFIELD SOFA IS PLACED BENEATH A PAIR OF WINDOWS TO THE RIGHT OF THE ALCOVE.

- BUTTON-TUFTED ARMCHAIRS ARE POSITIONED ALONGSIDE A THREE-TIERED MAHOGANY-AND-BRASS SIDE TABLE. THIS TABLE PROVIDES SPACE NEEDED FOR BOOKS AND OTHER READING MATERIALS, AND SERVES AS A PLACE TO REST A DRINK.

- CLUB CHAIRS ARE LOCATED IN THE MAIN SEATING AREA.

- A LARGE OCTAGONAL MAHOGANY PEDESTAL LIBRARY TABLE WITH GILT DECORATION SITS DIRECTLY ACROSS FROM THE PAIR OF ARMCHAIRS. A BUTTON-TUFTED OTTOMAN IN GREEN VELVET IS PLACED UNDERNEATH.

- WALL-TO-WALL CARPET PROVIDES A WEIGHTY AND SUITABLE ANCHOR TO THIS VERY TALL ROOM.

- THE SCOTTISH ORKNEY CHAIR OF RUSH AND OAK ADDS ADDITIONAL TEXTURE TO A PRIMARILY UPHOLSTERED ROOM.

- A LARGE WOVEN PLANTER HAND-PAINTED WITH A PASTORAL SCENE SITS BEHIND THE ORKNEY CHAIR.

- A ROUND TRIPOD TABLE SITS TO THE LEFT OF THE CHESTERFIELD SOFA WHILE ON THE RIGHT SIDE A SQUARE SOFA TABLE RESIDES.

STAGE II

OPULENT VELVET AND BULLION FRINGE ENHANCE THE ELEGANT NATURE OF THE ROOM. MEANWHILE, THE AMPLE SCALE OF THE TUFTED SOFA AND ARMCHAIRS MAKE IT QUITE OBVIOUS THAT COMFORT NEED NOT BE SACRIFICED FOR BEAUTY'S SAKE.

❧ NEEDLEPOINT AND FABRIC PILLOWS ARE ADDED TO THE SOFA, CHAIRS, AND WINDOW SEAT.

❧ THE WALLS ARE PAINTED SAGE GREEN, A COLOR REPEATED IN MOST OF THE ROOM'S UPHOLSTERY.

❧ A LARGE PORCELAIN JAR WITH A BLACK BACKGROUND PROVIDES A CENTERPIECE FOR THE OCTAGONAL TABLE AND BALANCES THE SCALE OF THE LAMPS PLACED ON THE OTHER TABLES. IN ROOMS OF THIS SIZE, LARGE-SCALE ITEMS ARE A NECESSITY.

❧ THE ARTWORK CONSISTS OF A PAIR OF LARGE AUDUBON PRINTS OF BIRDS (ONLY ONE IS VISIBLE) ON EITHER SIDE OF THE ENTRANCE TO THE ALCOVE AND A GROUP OF ENGLISH PASTORAL PAINTINGS.

❧ LARGE BRONZE URN LAMPS TOPPED WITH BEIGE SILK SHADES PROVIDE LIGHT ON EITHER SIDE OF THE SOFA.

❧ FOR CONTRAST, THE LAMP LOCATED ON THE TABLE IN FRONT OF THE ALCOVE IS TOPPED WITH A RED GATHERED SILK SHADE.

❧ FAVORITE BOOKS AND FAMILY PHOTO ALBUMS ARE STACKED ON THE LOWER SHELVES OF THE THREE-TIERED TABLE FOR EASY ACCESS.

STAGE III

L IGHT POURS INTO THE BRIGHTLY-COLORED ROOM THROUGH THE TAILORED PLAID SHADES, MAKING THIS ROOM FEEL MUCH COZIER THAN MOST ROOMS OF ITS SIZE. THE ROOM CAN SERVE AS AN IDEAL ESCAPE FOR A LONE READER SITTING ON THE CUSHIONED WINDOW SEAT OR CAN ACCOMMODATE A MUCH LARGER GROUP IN THE OPEN MAIN SEATING AREA.

❧ ADDITIONAL DECORATIVE OBJECTS, PHOTOS, PLANTS, ARTWORK, AND, ESPECIALLY, THE TALL TREE INJECT THIS ROOM WITH LIFE.

❧ SIMPLE ROMAN SHADES WERE SELECTED TO KEEP THE ROOM FROM BECOMING FUSSY AND TO AVOID COMPETING WITH THE ARCHITECTURE.

❧ MAGAZINES AND MORE BOOKS AWAIT THEIR READERS.

❧ A LARGE CARRIAGE CLOCK IS NOW PLACED ON THE ROUND TABLE IN FRONT OF THE ALCOVE.

❧ A SELECT FEW FAMILY PHOTOS ARE PLACED ON TABLES IN THE ALCOVE AREA AND NEXT TO THE COUCH.

"*This was . . . the room of someone who had chosen every
particle of furniture with great care, so that each chair,
each vase, each small infinitesimal thing should be
in harmony with one another.*" —DAPHNE DU MAURIER

Variations

*P*LAID SHADES FINISHED WITH TAB HEMS AND
SECURED ON A ROD ARE HUNG IN THE ALCOVE.
THE IKAT FABRIC ON THE WINDOW-SEAT CUSHION,
ALONG WITH A MIXTURE OF PLAID AND IKAT PIL-
LOWS, CREATES A SOFT AND HARMONIOUS CORNER.

*M*AHOGANY BLINDS WITH A WIDE GREEN TAPE
TRIM PROVIDE TEXTURAL INTEREST AND HIGH
CONTRAST TO THESE WINDOWS. IN A LARGE-SCALE
ROOM THE HEAVINESS OF THE WOODEN BLINDS IS
NOT A FACTOR.

One of the most notable features of this living room is the number and height of the windows. As the room is not a formal one, curtains, however simple, might still overpower the room by the sheer volume of fabric required. Here are four window treatments that confine themselves to inside the window frame.

A TAILORED SHADE IS CREATED WITH A SOLID GREEN FABRIC AND CONTRASTING CREAM TAPE. LARGE WINDOWS ON A GRAND SCALE CAN HANDLE A DARK COLOR.

*T*HE IKAT FABRIC IS USED HERE TO CREATE ANOTHER KIND OF TAILORED SHADE WITH TRIM IN A SOLID BULLION FRINGE, WHICH ANCHORS THIS TREATMENT AND GIVES IT SUBSTANCE. THIS TYPE OF TREATMENT SOFTENS THE STRONG LINES OF THE WINDOWS AND THE ROOM WITHOUT CREATING AN OVERDRESSED APPEARANCE. THE SHAPED BOTTOM OF THIS TREATMENT TAKES YOUR EYE OFF THE LONG VERTICAL LINES CREATED BY THE WINDOWS.

A DICTIONARY OF DETAILS

UPHOLSTERY

"I cannot conceive of any room that is to be lived in today without the use of upholstered furniture. The late nineteenth century brought this great luxury to us and we have never ceased enjoying it, and most of our lives sitting on it."

—BILLY BALDWIN

To me, nothing looks more inviting than a room with comfortable and "well-dressed" furniture. Upholstered furniture, when treated as a key ingredient in decorating, can also virtually transform a room.

Choosing upholstery is truly a matter of personal taste. Yet in my experiences as an interior designer, I have also tried to follow a few basic rules:

⚜ Fabric chosen for upholstery should support the rest of your scheme—draperies, carpet, etc.

⚜ Analyze the amount of use each piece will receive. Durable fabrics such as velvet, brocade, tapestry, damask, linen, ticking stripe, and plain and printed cottons such as chintz are your most likely candidates for upholstered furniture.

⚜ Large upholstered pieces become more conspicuous in large bold prints and bright colors.

⚜ To make upholstered furniture less conspicuous, duplicate fabrics within the room and/or select a fabric that harmonizes with the carpet.

Until the beginning of the seventeenth century, the usual way to make a seat comfortable was to lay a cushion on it. The development of comfort in upholstered furniture appears to have begun with the "sleeping chair," or easy chair. The great luxury of these late-seventeenth-century furnishings came with the use of huge down-filled seat cushions set in wells surrounded by rolls of padding in the underseat. Yet it was the edge roll that was crucial to the evolution of the upholstery shape. Craftsmen quickly realized that it could be used not only to help attach the cushion to the base but also to shape and support stuffing within a fixed cover, creating an ideal sitting chair. By the end of the eighteenth century, chair design had reached its zenith. Form and function became truly united in that century's great examples of superb line, proportion, upholstery expertise, and comfort.

Here is a brief glossary of upholstery trimmings that should help you to describe and identify various styles as you find the one that's right for you:

❧ PIPING or CORD is one of the simplest trimmings and serves to outline and emphasize the overall shape of the piece. By using a contrasting piping or cord you can further emphasize the configuration of your chair.

❧ GIMPS are narrow flat woven trims, and braids are tightly woven flat bands that can also be used for accentuation of shape.

❧ FRINGE can be simple, like bullion fringe, or ornately tasseled and made from a wide variety of fibers. Fringe is usually used as a skirt finish and is made in a variety of lengths and thicknesses.

❧ TASSELS, large or small, add flair to strategic points of upholstery, cushions, and bolsters, serving no other function than to decorate and entertain.

❧ Finally, don't forget the vast variety of grosgrain, woven and velvet ribbons, and flat tapes that can be used around the bottom of a chair skirt, either individually or in combination with others.

UPHOLSTERY

A CHAIR SKIRT BOXED AND SELF-PIPED WITH A DROP RUFFLE AND A MATCHING CIRCULAR BACK COVER. THE SEAT COVER CAN BE CLOSED WITH BOWS, BUTTONS, OR VELCRO.

A LARGE-CHECK CHAIR SKIRT WITH A DEEP RUFFLE.

A SLIPCOVER WITH A KNOTTED SASH IN THE BACK. THE FOLDS OF THE FABRIC RESEMBLE CONSTRUCTION USED IN DRESSMAKING.

A SHIELD-BACK CHAIR SLIPCOVERED IN A TAILORED
BOX-PLEATED CHAIR SKIRT.

A CHAIR SKIRT FINISHED IN A ZIGZAG HEM WITH TASSEL
EMBELLISHMENTS.

*"A chair is a very difficult object.
A skyscraper is almost easier. That is why
Chippendale is famous."*

—MIES VAN DER ROHE

A CHAIR SKIRT SLIPCOVER WITH A DROPPED RUFFLE TRIM.

UPHOLSTERY

A CHAIR SKIRT WITH A LARGE FLOUNCE FINISHED WITH
A TWO-TIERED RUFFLE TRIM.

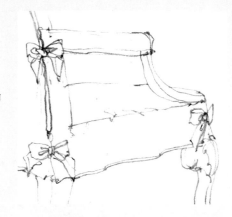

A SLIPCOVER FOR AN ARMCHAIR WITH BOW CLOSURES THAT CAN
BE DONE IN THE SAME FABRIC OR CONTRASTING FABRIC.

*S*HIRRED FABRIC EDGES THE UPHOLSTERED CUSHIONS ON THIS
CHAIR. FLORAL INSERTS APPEAR ON THE SEAT AND THE BACK.
THEY ALSO COULD BE DONE WITH PIECES OF ANTIQUE FABRIC
OR WITH A SIMILAR YET CONTRASTING FABRIC, OR THE ENTIRE
CHAIR COULD BE DONE IN THE SAME FABRIC.

LARGE SILK TASSELS FINISH THE FRONTS OF THE ARMS ON THIS SOFA, UPHOLSTERED IN A SOLID FABRIC WITH CONTRASTING SILK ROPE TRIM. IN LIEU OF A SKIRT, DEEP SILK FRINGE WITH A BRAIDED HEADING IS USED.

A SINGLE PANEL INSERT RUNS FROM THE BACK OF THE CHAIR THROUGH THE SEAT. THE SKIRT IS GATHERED AND EDGED IN A COMPLEMENTARY PRINT OR TAPE.

AN ELABORATE SILK FRINGE DONE IN A ZIGZAG FORM CREATES A SKIRT FOR THIS UPHOLSTERED ARMCHAIR.

A SCALLOP-EDGED SLIPCOVER FINISHED WITH CONTRASTING PIPING TO EMPHASIZE THE DEEP SCALLOPS AND THE SHAPE OF THE BACK.

UPHOLSTERY

A SLIPCOVER WITH A SCALLOPED EDGE ACCENTED WITH A FLAT SILK RIBBON TRIM.

A SLIPCOVER EXECUTED IN A HORIZONTAL STRIPE FABRIC WITH CONTRASTING FABRIC BOWS.

A SLIPCOVER WITH A DEEP FLOUNCE AND SMALL BOW ATTACHMENTS AT THE BACK.

A LOOSE-FITTING SLIPCOVER DRESSES THIS PLUMP SOFA. THE FABRIC IS A WIDE STRIPE. THE CORNER PLEATED SKIRT IS FINISHED WITH THE SAME FABRIC CUT ON THE BIAS.

*T*HIS CHAIR SKIRT IS DONE IN A SIMPLE BOX PLEAT WITH A DOUBLE ROW OF APPLIED FLAT RIBBON, IN A CONTRASTING COLOR. AS AN OPTION, GIMP OR TAPE CAN ALSO BE USED.

*T*ASSELS EMPHASIZE THE SCALLOPS IN THIS CHAIR'S ELABORATE SKIRT. THE UNDERSKIRT IS FINISHED WITH A BULLION TRIM.

*C*ONTRASTING ROPE TRIM COORDINATES NICELY WITH THE DEEP BULLION FRINGE USED IN LIEU OF A SKIRT.

PILLOWS

Pillows provide comfort as well as an often needed decorative punch on an otherwise uninviting chair or sofa. The variations in construction and styling are virtually limitless. Fabrics, shapes, sizes, trims, and combinations of trims present possibilities that are only limited by the constraints of one's purse! Furniture that might appear uninteresting on a showroom floor may take on a totally new life with the addition of the right pillows.

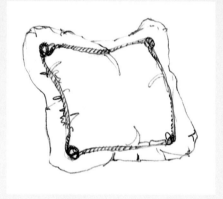

A PILLOW WITH A SELF-RUFFLE AND CONTRASTING SILK ROPE TRIM KNOTTED IN THE CORNERS.

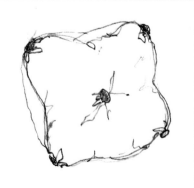

A TURKISH-CORNERED PILLOW WITH A SINGLE CENTER BUTTON AND BUTTONS AT EACH CORNER.

A PILLOW WITH CONTRASTING SILK ROPE TRIM AND A GREEK KEY PATTERN IN THE GUSSET.

A PILLOW WITH TURKISH CORNERS AND CONTRASTING ROPE TRIM.

> *"A comfortable house is a great source of happiness. It ranks immediately after health and a good conscience."*
> —THE REVEREND SYDNEY SMITH

A SELF-RUFFLE PILLOW SLIPCOVER WITH BUTTON CLOSURES AND RUFFLE TRIM CUT ON THE BIAS.

Pillows

A SIMPLE PILLOW SLIPCOVER WITH DECORATIVE BOW TIES.

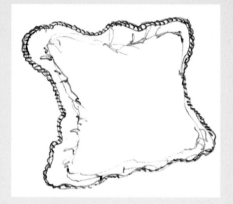

A SELF-RUFFLE PILLOW WITH SILK ROPE TRIM EMPHASIZING THE EDGE OF THE RUFFLE.

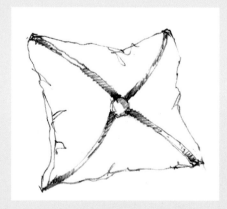

*A*N ENVELOPE PILLOW WITH A CENTRAL BUTTON DETAIL.

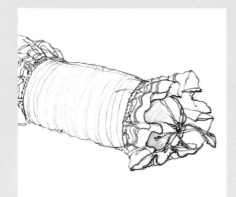

A NECK ROLL WITH CONTRASTING LACE-TRIMMED RUFFLES AND A DRAWSTRING CLOSURE

A BOLSTER PILLOW WITH BUTTON-FINISHED ENDS EXECUTED IN A STRIPED FABRIC.

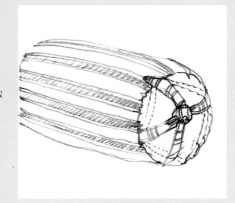

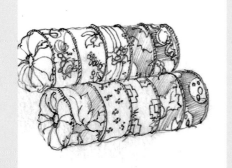

A PAIR OF BOLSTER PILLOWS CREATED FROM VARIOUS PATTERNED FABRICS. PLEATED ENDS ARE FINISHED WITH BUTTONS. EACH SECTION IS OUTLINED WITH THE SAME ROPE DETAIL.

A SMOCKED, KNIFE-EDGED PILLOW.

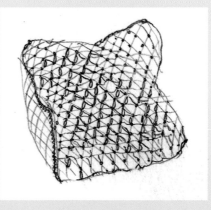

PILLOWS

A KNIFE-EDGED PILLOW TUFTED WITH FOUR BOWS AND TRIMMED WITH CONTRASTING ROPE TRIM.

A TAPESTRY-INSET PILLOW WITH DIAGONAL-CHECK PANELS AND SILK BRAID TRIM SEGREGATING THE VARIOUS PATTERNS.

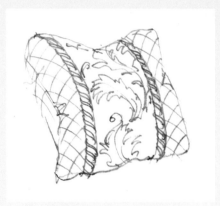

A PATCHWORK PILLOW DONE IN A CONCENTRIC-SQUARE STYLE.

RIBBONS AND BOWS EMBELLISH THIS SIMPLE PILLOW COVERED IN A SOLID VELVET.

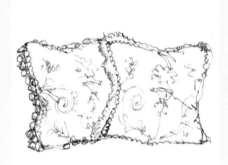

ANTIQUE TAPESTRY PILLOWS FINISHED IN SILK FRINGE (RIGHT) AND BALL FRINGE (LEFT).

A SELF-RUFFLE AND SELF-PIPED PILLOW WITH A HAND-PAINTED FLORAL DESIGN.

A PATCHWORK PILLOW DONE IN VARIOUS FABRICS AND TEXTURES. THE CROSS-STITCHING ENHANCES THE CONCEPT OF THE PATCHWORK.

PILLOWS

A FLORAL-PATTERNED PILLOW WITH A PINKED GATHERED RUFFLE.

TAPESTRY PILLOWS WITH SILK ROPE TRIM AND CORNERS EMBELLISHED IN VARIOUS LOOP DESIGNS.

A PILLOW WITH FABRIC ROSETTES FINISHING THE TURKISH CORNERS.

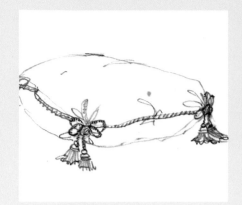

A PILLOW FINISHED WITH SILK ROPE TRIM CULMINATING IN TASSELS AND BOWS AT THE GATHERED CORNERS.

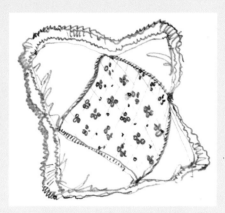

A PINKED RUFFLE FINISHES THIS PILLOW WITH A SMALL FLORAL DIAMOND INSET.

"As regards to decoration, I want you only to consult your own natural choice and liking."

—JOHN RUSKIN

LAMPSHADES

Lampshades affect the amount of light emitted from your fixture. Give consideration to the amount of light needed in a certain area before selecting your shade. Opaque paper or metal shades emit light at the top and bottom. Translucent shades—silk or cotton shades, for example—emit light up, down, and through the shade.

❀ It is essential that the shade cover the entire brass socket.

❀ An elaborate base should have a plain shade, while a plain base can take a more elaborate shade.

❀ Before choosing a fabric to make a lampshade, first hold the fabric up to an illuminated lightbulb. The look and color you want is determined by how the fabric appears with light behind it—not as it appears when held in one's hand or on a scheme board.

To EMPHASIZE THE SCALLOP, THIS SHADE IS FINISHED WITH A TWO-TIERED SILK FRINGE AND CONTRASTING SILK ROPE TRIM.

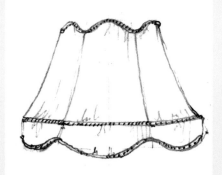

SILK MINI-ROPE TRIM FINISHES THIS CHIMNEY-SHAPED SHADE.

Silk fringe and a silk rope trim done in a loop pattern are used to trim this knife-pleated shade.

This bell-shaped chintz shade has its fabric stretched to highlight its pattern. It is outlined with gimp at the bottom and the top.

"It has long been an axiom of mine that the little things are definitely the most important."

—Sherlock Holmes

This hexagonal scalloped shade has a base with a contrasting cuff and silk fringe. Note that each section is convex.

LAMPSHADES

THIS SHIRRED SILK SHADE IS OUTLINED WITH A SET-IN RUFFLE AT THE TOP AND BOTTOM.

A PLEATED EMPIRE SHADE HAS A ROW OF SMOCKING AT THE BASE AND AT THE TOP.

THIS BOX-PLEATED EMPIRE SHADE IS FINISHED WITH A SMOCKED CUFF.

A BUTTERFLY RUFFLE FINISHES THIS SILK GATHERED SHADE.

*T*HIS EMPIRE SHADE IS FINISHED IN A TWO-COLORED SILK FRINGE AT THE BOTTOM AND COORDINATING TAPE AT THE TOP.

"Genius begins where rules end."

—SIR JOSHUA REYNOLDS

*H*ERE A SHADE IS MADE BY STRETCHING THE FABRIC OVER THE FRAME AND HIGHLIGHTING ITS SHAPE WITH CONTRAST-ING TRIM.

LAMPSHADES

A KNIFE-PLEATED HEXAGONAL SHADE IS FINISHED WITH
A FRINGE AND A CRISSCROSS DECORATIVE TRIM.

A SIMPLE PARCHMENT SHADE DONE IN A PYRAMID SHAPE.
THIS SHAPE IS SUITABLE FOR A NUMBER OF MATERIALS.

*A*N ACCORDION-PLEATED SHADE IS FINISHED WITH A
RIBBON-AND-BOW DRAWSTRING.

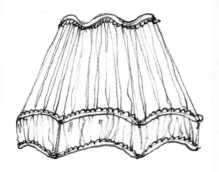

A REVERSE SCALLOP-EDGED SHADE IS KNIFE-PLEATED AND FINISHED WITH A SILK LOOP TRIM.

THIS PLEATED SHADE HAS A SMOCKED CUFF AT THE TOP AND BOTTOM AND IS FINISHED IN A SILK FRINGE.

"The first rule of decoration is that you can break almost all the other rules."

—BILLY BALDWIN

EACH SECTION IS CONCAVE IN THIS OCTAGONAL SHADE, PLEATED AND SMOCKED AT THE TOP AND BOTTOM AND FINISHED WITH A SILK TRIM.

LAMPSHADES

*T*HIS CARD SHADE IS HAND-PAINTED WITH A FLORAL PAT-
TERN. SIMPLE CARD SHADES ALLOW YOU THE OPPORTUNITY
TO PERSONALIZE BY PAINTING A MOTIF TO WORK WITH YOUR
SCHEME.

*H*ERE A HEXAGONAL STRETCHED-SILK SHADE IS FINISHED
WITH A CUFF AND TRIM IN THE SAME FABRIC.

*S*ILK ROPE TRIM HIGHLIGHTS THE DEEP SCALLOPS OF THIS
PLEATED SILK SHADE.

SOURCES

Laura Ashley Home Furnishings (MO, R)
1300 MacArthur Boulevard
Mahwah, NJ 07430
(800) 367-2000
*Decorative accessories, furniture, lighting, curtains and
shades, linens, home fragrance, tableware, etc.*

Brunschwig & Fils (T)
Suite 1120
979 Third Avenue
New York, NY 10022
(212) 838-7878
Fabric, wallpaper, and trim

Calico Corners (R)
203 Gale Lane
Kennett Square, PA 19348
(610) 444-9700
Fabrics and fabrication service

Carver's Guild (T)
Cannery Row
P.O. Box 198
West Groton, MA 01472
(800) 445-3464
Mirrors

Chambers (MO)
P.O. Box 7841
San Francisco, CA 94120-7841
(800) 334-9790
*Decorative accessories, furniture, lighting, curtains and
shades, linens, home fragrance, tableware, etc.*

Chelsea House Port Royal (T)
230 Linwood Road, Box 399
Gastonia, NC 28052
(704) 867-5929
*Lamps, chandeliers, paintings and prints, furniture,
porcelain, silver, brackets, and other decorative
accessories*

R = Retail, MO = Mail Order Catalog, T = To the trade only

*Sources that sell to the trade only will happily provide the names
of retail distributors upon request.*

Clarence House Imports (T)
Suite 105
979 Third Avenue
New York, NY 10022
(212) 752-2890
Fabric, wallpaper, and trim

Crate and Barrel (MO, R)
P.O. Box 9059
Wheeling, IL 60090-9059
(800) 323-5461
*Decorative accessories, furniture, lighting, curtains and
shades, linens, home fragrance, tableware, etc.*

Faroy (T)
6937 Flintlock
Houston, TX 77040
(800) 256-5689
Decorative accessories

Great City Traders (T)
537 Stevenson
San Francisco, CA 94103-1636
(415) 863-9930
*Lighting, mirrors, candlesticks, boxes, and other
accessories*

Hickory Chair Company (T)
P.O. Box 2147
Hickory, NC 28603
(704) 328-1801
Furniture and upholstery

The Horchow Home Collection (MO)
P.O. Box 620048
Dallas, TX 75262-0048
(800) 527-0303
*Decorative accessories, furniture, lighting, curtains and
shades, linens, home fragrance, tableware, etc.*

Christopher Hyland, Inc. (T)
Suite 1710
979 Third Avenue
New York NY 10022
(212) 688-6121
Fabric, wallpaper, trim, lighting, and accessories

Lee Jofa (T)
Suite 234
979 Third Avenue
New York, NY 10022
(212) 688-0444
Fabric, wallpaper, and trim

Benjamin Moore (T)
51 Chestnut Ridge Road
Montvale, NJ 07645
(800) 672-4686
Paint

Mottahedeh (T)
1400 Honeyspot Road. Ext.
Stratford, CT 06497
(800) 443-8225
*Porcelain tableware and accessories, silver and brass
accessory items*

Peel and Company (T)
4240 Hwy 22, #6
Mandeville, LA 70448
(504) 674-0087
Needlepoint rugs and pillows

Pier One Imports (R)
P.O. Box 96102
Forth Worth, TX 76161-0020
(800) 245-4595
Pillows, tableware, furniture, accessories, lighting

Polo Ralph Lauren (R)
867 Madison Avenue
New York, NY 10021
(212) 606-2100
*Pillows, fabrics, wallpaper, tableware, linens, furniture,
fragrance*

Pottery Barn (MO, R)
P.O. Box 7044
San Francisco, CA 94120-7044
(800) 922-5507
*Decorative accessories, furniture, lighting, curtains and
shades, linens, home fragrance, tableware, etc.*

Reed and Barton (T)
144 West Britannia Street
Taunton, MA 02780
(800) 822-1824
Silver picture frames and accessories

Rosecore Carpet Co. (T)
Suite 1002
979 Third Avenue
New York, NY 10022
(212) 421-7272
Carpet

Saxony Carpet Company, Inc. (T)
979 Third Avenue
Suite 932
New York, NY 10022
(212) 755-7100
Carpet

Scalamandre (T)
950 Third Avenue
New York, NY 10022
(718) 361-8500
Fabric, wallpaper, trim, and carpets

F. Schumacher & Company (T)
939 Third Avenue
New York, NY 10022
(800) 332-3384
Fabric, wallpaper, trim, and carpets

Smith and Hawken (MO, R)
2 Arbor Lane
P.O. Box 6900
Florence, KY 41022
(800) 776-3333
*Decorative accessories, furniture, lighting, curtains and
shades, linens, home fragrance, tableware, etc.*

Stark Concepts (T)
Suite 1102
979 Third Avenue
New York, NY 10022
(212) 752-9000
Carpet

Two's Company (T)
33 Bertel Avenue
Mount Vernon, NJ 10550-4616
(800) 431-1160
Decorative accessories

Waverly (T,R)
939 Third Avenue
New York, NY 10022
(800) 423-5881
Fabric and wallpaper

ROOM SCHEME DETAILS

A FORMAL DINING ROOM WITH A VIEW TO THE GARDEN

PAINT
> Benjamin Moore "Off White"

FABRIC
> Schumacher "Taveta Moiré Stripe" (#57276), in citrine
> Schumacher "Stowe Texture" (#92966), in raspberry
> Schumacher "September" (#56000), in natural
> Brunschwig & Fils "Frange Torse Rope on Tape" (#90540) on dining-chair cushions, color #37 ("Fontainebleau")
> Brunschwig & Fils five-inch "Frange Torse Fringe" (#90336) on window treatments, color #30 ("Liberty")

AN INTIMATE DINING ROOM WITH A SWEDISH ACCENT

PAINT
> Benjamin Moore yellow (#296)
> Benjamin Moore eggshell white (#968)
> Benjamin Moore pale yellow (#928)

FABRIC
> Schumacher "Belle De Crecy" (#163703), in pink
> Schumacher "William and Mary Diamond" (#56260), in natural
> Schumacher six-inch "Edouard" bullion fringe (#891440) on curtains, in alabaster
> Rosecore "Bellary" #15 coir carpet

A WARM SITTING ROOM/LIBRARY

PAINT
> Benjamin Moore ocher (#319)
> Benjamin Moore ivory (#932)

FABRIC
> Schumacher "William and Mary Diamond" (#56260), in natural
> Schumacher "Gloucester Adaptation Damask" (#52842), in coral
> Schumacher "Monarque Imberline" (#56190), in red
> Stark "Dalkeith" carpet, in blue
> Schumacher six-inch "Eduoard" bullion fringe (#891440) on slipper chairs, in alabaster
> Lee Jofa "Frange Torse" 4³/4-inch bullion fringe (#834955) on windows, in sienne antique
> Christopher Hyland five-inch fringe with netting and tassels (#AC110) on table skirt
> Clarence House "Cyrano-Frange Moulinee" (#CY224/2001) on table skirt, in gold/blue/rose

A COLORFUL ROOM FOR LIVING

PAINT
> Benjamin Moore periwinkle (#1380)
> Benjamin Moore "China White"

FABRIC
> Schumacher "Meredith" (#166560), in robin's-egg blue
> Schumacher "Josephine's Gingham" (#166361), in pink
> Schumacher "Montfort Check" (#161114), in aqua
> Schumacher "Cross Town Plaid" (#57083), in aqua and bone
> Schumacher "Gretchen" (#56572), in willow
> Schumacher "Stowe Texture" (#92961), in spruce
> Rosecore "Winslow" carpet, in green
> Brunschwig & Fils "Orion Cord on Tape" (#90499) on sofa and pillows, color # 5

A SUNNY AND SOPHISTICATED LIVING ROOM

PAINT
> Benjamin Moore beige (#949 and #949 flat)

FABRIC
> Waverly "Town and Country Velvet" (#602789), in acorn
> Schumacher "Oatlands Leaf" (#165025), in taupe
> Schumacher "Gretchen" (#56579), in henna
> Schumacher "Chartres Linen Damask" (#57423), in pink
> Schumacher "Takahara" (#513781), in tan
> Schumacher "Wilton Hollow" (#167142), in cream and fern
> Stark "Fila Grane et Fleur" carpet
> Brunschwig & Fils eight-inch "Frange Torse Fringe" (#90537) on ottoman, color #37

Lee Jofa 7⅞-inch "Frange Torse" bullion fringe
    (#834952A) on banquettes, in "cordage"

A NEW ANGLE IN THE MASTER BEDROOM

PAINT
    Benjamin Moore "Decorator's White"

FABRIC
    Schumacher "Attedorn" (#42976), in ivy
    Schumacher "Williamsburg Moiré" (#165135), in
        jade
    Schumacher "Gretchen" (#56578, #56576, and
        #56571), in red, delft, and green
    Schumacher "Captiva" (#57082), in red and blue
    Schumacher "Parrot Tulips" (#167190), in white
        and multi
    Schumacher "Rowallane" wallpaper (#507841), in
        china blue
    Rosecore "Flower Petal" carpet from "The Wilton
        Collection," in mint on white
    Scalamandre 5½-inch bullion fringe (#FB1067-1)
        on curtains

A SOOTHING MASTER BEDROOM SUITE

PAINT
    Benjamin Moore beige (#HC-26)
    Benjamin Moore white (#970)

FABRIC
    Schumacher "Brittany Vine" (#166395), in camel
    Schumacher "Chartres Linen Damask" (#57420),
        in sand
    Schumacher "Williamsburg Moiré" (#165131), in
        moonstone
    Schumacher "Keswick Plaid" (#57310), in green
    Tasitweed "Tasitex 4400" sisal carpet, color #3400
        (amberspice)

A GENTLEMAN'S LIBRARY/RETREAT

PAINT
    Benjamin Moore beige (#982)
    Benjamin Moore taupe (#984)
    Benjamin Moore "China White"

FABRIC
    Schumacher "Sur la Rive" (#28230), in black
    Schumacher "Canterbury Check" (#92505), in
        black and white
    Schumacher "Rouen" (#56844), in black
    Schumacher "William and Mary Diamond"
        (#56260), in natural
    Schumacher "Gretchen" (#56582), in charcoal
    Schumacher "Yorkshire Plaid" (#56990), in black
        and taupe
    Chelsea House leather trim on bookshelf

A SUN-FILLED FAMILY PORCH

PAINT
    Benjamin Moore celadon (#457)
    Benjamin Moore cream (#876)

FABRIC
    Schumacher "Toile Orientale" (#165090), in
        document red
    Schumacher "Chatelet Diamonds" (#91695), in
        rouge
    Schumacher "Piastrella" (#56476), in ruby
    Schumacher "Diamonte" (#56414), in red
    Schumacher "Nelly's Quilt" (#56135), in
        apple
    Rosecore "Seagrass" carpet

AN ARCHITECTURALLY INSPIRED LIVING ROOM

PAINT
    Benjamin Moore sage green (#HC-118)
    Benjamin Moore "Bone White"
    Benjamin Moore "Bone White Flat"

FABRIC
    Schumacher "Gainsborough Velvet" (#42873), in
        willow
    Schumacher "Lilly Ikat Stripe" (#165180), in
        document coral and leaf
    Schumacher "Keswick Plaid" (#57313), in terra
        cotta and green
    Saxony "Darby" carpet, in rust (#2)
    Schumacher "Claude" eight-inch bullion fringe
        (#891466) on armchairs and ottoman, in
        celadon

Decoration aside, isn't it an undefinable atmosphere,
attitude, or aura that we seek when we strive to make *our* house *our* home—
an intimate atmosphere that immediately speaks
to us and says, "Make yourself at home"?
With this bit of advice I must now leave you on
your own to finish the job.

Enjoy the process.

Charlotte Moss